THE FIRST WORLD WAR

IAN CAWOOD and DAVID McKINNON-BELL

ROUTLEDGE

London and New York

First published 2001
by Routledge
11 New Fetter Lane, London EC4P 4EE

Simultaneously published in the USA and Canada
by Routledge
29 West 35th Street, New York, NY 10001

Routledge is an imprint of the Taylor & Francis Group

© 2001 Ian Cawood and David McKinnon-Bell

Typeset in Akzidenz Grotesk and Perpetua by
Keystroke, Jacaranda Lodge, Wolverhampton
Printed and bound in Great Britain by
TJ International, Padstow, Cornwall

British Library Cataloguing in Publication Data
A catalogue record for this book is available from the British Library

Library of Congress Cataloging in Publication Data
Cawood, Ian.
    The First World War / Ian Cawood and David McKinnon-Bell.
        p. cm. – (Questions and analysis in history)
    Includes bibliographical references and index.
        1. World War, 1914–1918. I. McKinnon-Bell, David. II. Title. III. Series.

D521 .C437 2000
940.3–dc21   00-024298

ISBN 0–415–22276–1

CONTENTS

SERIES PREFACE

Most history textbooks now aim to provide the student with interpretation, and many also cover the historiography of a topic. Some include a selection of sources.

So far, however, there have been few attempts to combine *all* the skills needed by the history student. Interpretation is usually found within an overall narrative framework and it is often difficult to separate the two for essay purposes. Where sources are included, there is rarely any guidance as to how to answer the questions on them.

The Questions and Analysis series is therefore based on the belief that another approach should be added to those which already exist. It has two main aims.

The first is to separate narrative from interpretation so that the latter is no longer diluted by the former. Most chapters start with a background narrative section containing essential information. This material is then used in a section focusing on analysis through a specific question. The main purpose of this is to help to tighten up essay technique.

The second aim is to provide a comprehensive range of sources for each of the issues covered. The questions are of the type which appear on examination papers, and some have worked answers to demonstrate the techniques required.

The chapters may be approached in different ways. The background narratives can be read first to provide an overall perspective, followed by the analyses and then the sources. The alternative method is to work through all the components of each chapter before going on to the next.

ACKNOWLEDGEMENTS

The author and publisher are grateful to the following for permission to reproduce copyright material:

For permission to include 'The Dead Statesman' by Rudyard Kipling, A.P. Watt Ltd on behalf of The National Trust for Places of Historic Interest or Natural Beauty. For *Goodbye to All That* by Robert Graves, by permission of Carcanet Press Ltd. Richard Pipes: *The Russian Revolution*. First published in 1990 in America by Alfred A. Knopf and in Great Britain by The Harvill Press. Copyright © Richard Pipes, 1990. Reproduced by permission of The Harvill Press. *Germany after the First World War* by Richard Bessel, © Richard Bessel 1993, by permission of Oxford University Press. An extract from *Imperial Germany and the Great War* by R. Chickering, 1993, by permission of Cambridge University Press. An extract from *The Upheaval of War* by J. Winter, 1988, by permission of Cambridge University Press. An extract from *The Deluge* by Arthur Marwick, 1991, by permission of Macmillan Press Ltd. *Mein Kampf* by Adolf Hitler by permission of Pimlico.

INTRODUCTION

Although the Great War of 1914–1918 is usually referred to as 'World War One', this can be a somewhat misleading title, not least because it implies that it was inconclusive, requiring World War Two to finally resolve matters. Also, unlike World War Two, the Great War was not an entirely global affair. Unarguably countries across the globe participated, and the conflict drew in the colonial and dependent territories of the European powers, from New Zealand to the Falklands. Similarly, fighting took place in Asia, Africa and almost all the world's oceans, but the majority of fighting and dying took place in Europe. Rather than being a war fought across the world, the Great War affected the world, due to its duration and the subsequent cost in lives, materials and trading opportunities to the participants. But what makes the Great War distinctive is not simply its scale, but that the degree of effort required from the chief participants to fight and win or lose the war, was unprecedented. The Great War has been described as the first 'Total War', forcing the powers to mobilise their societies and economies on an until then undreamed of scale. This book is therefore not primarily concerned with the military campaigns themselves and the soldiers' immediate experience of fighting, though they form the background to any analysis, rather it intends to compare the impact of the Great War on the four major European powers of 1914: France, Britain, Germany and Russia. This comparative approach is taken because, as Jay Winter has put it, 'the history of the

Great War has been told time and again within a national framework. Almost all students of the period have been imprisoned, to a greater or lesser degree, within this framework of analysis.'[1] The book focuses particularly on the economic, social and political effects of the war on these Great Powers, and attempts to use this as a means to understand why Russia and Germany lost the war and why Britain and France won it, and to set the Great War in broader historical context in order to understand its importance in challenging the global balance of power in ways that are still felt almost a century later. Put simply, we want students to understand why the Great War of 1914–18 is, in effect, the pivotal event of what Eric Hobsbawm has called 'the short twentieth century'.[2]

1

THE OUTBREAK OF WAR

BACKGROUND NARRATIVE

As every student knows, Archduke Franz Ferdinand, the heir to the Austro-Hungarian throne, and his wife, Sophie, were shot and killed by the Bosnian Serb terrorist Gavrilo Princip on 28 June 1914. Popular feeling in Austria and Germany took the form of riots and the destruction of Serb businesses, but the Austrian government saw it as an opportunity to crush Serbia, whose enlargement following the Balkan Wars of 1912 and 1913 blocked Austria's attempted expansion into the east, and whose championing of Slav independence threatened to destabilise the multi-racial composition of the polyglot Austro-Hungarian Empire. Austria's delay in asking redress of the Serbs was caused by her need to consult with Germany, her chief ally since 1879. The resulting German guarantee of full support for any action that Austria might take, on 5 July (the so-called 'blank cheque'), has convinced many historians, most notably Fritz Fischer, that Germany was inciting Austria to act and thus precipitate a European war.[1] Whatever the truth of this, Serbia's refusal to agree to all of Austria's excessive demands led to Austria declaring war on Serbia on 28 July and resulted in the fatal acceleration of the 'July Crisis'. First, Russia came to Serbia's assistance, mobilising her vast army, then Germany, conscious that she faced enemies on two fronts, declared war on Russia and invaded France, who would be able to put an army in the field first, in accordance with the Schlieffen Plan. In order to defeat France quickly, Germany invaded through Belgium, breaching Belgian neutrality, and thus gave Britain good reason to enter the war on France's side. Although unenthusiastic, Asquith's Liberal government recognised that, in defending Belgium, Britain was protecting her national interests, and, thereby, preventing Germany from dominating the continent.

A clichéd view of the reaction to the outbreak of war, encouraged by the governments of the powers, sees popular support throughout Europe. Images of cheering crowds, attacks on enemy foreigners and masses of eager conscripts and volunteers seem to bear witness to this. But it would be a mistake to assume that all Europe responded in this fashion. Those who saw the war as an interruption in a fight for equality, such as some members of the women's suffrage movement and, most notably, many leading socialists, believed that the ruling classes had deliberately sought conflict to distract popular support away from them. Jean Jaurès, the leader of the French Socialists, said as much and was murdered by a 'patriot' on 31 July. The elderly, with their memories of the previous conflicts, such as the Franco-Prussian War of 1870–1, the Boer War of 1899–1902 and the Russo-Japanese War of 1904–5, were far less enthusiastic, and it seems that reaction in the towns, with the swiftness of news, rumour and excitement, was more positive on the whole than in the countryside, where people faced the prospect of 1914's harvest being disrupted by the departure of young men and the ravages of marching troops. Even in the cities, the initial enthusiasm was hardly universal, and often did not survive the autumn.

In part the 'mood of 1914' stemmed from a naive belief in every state that the war would be brief and that one's own military prowess would inevitably triumph within months. Everything would be 'over by Christmas'. This is evident in popular misconceptions about the nature of the coming conflict as much as in the inadequate preparations made by the governments of Europe. The French military commander Foch once remarked that 'every war is fought on the basis of the last one'. However, the war that began in Europe in 1914 was so wholly unlike the previous European conflicts in the 1860s and 1870s that every preparation made on the basis of these experiences proved inadequate within months.

ANALYSIS (1): WERE THE GREAT POWERS ECONOMICALLY AND MILITARILY PREPARED FOR WAR?

By 1914, Germany, having experienced a spectacular industrial revolution, was rapidly overhauling Britain as Europe's foremost industrial power. Germany's industrial achievements were impressive. GNP grew by 600 per cent during the Imperial era. In 1913, she mined 277 million tons of coal – second only to Britain. She milled more steel than Britain, France and Russia combined. Giant German cartels like Siemens and AEG dominated European electrical markets. German chemicals consortia produced most of the world's dyes and industrial acids. Overall Germany exported nearly as much as Britain.[2]

Alongside this, her population had increased from 49 million in 1890 to 66 million in 1913, second only to Russia among the European powers. Furthermore, industrial development had been accompanied by the evolution of an excellent rail network and canal system, and a huge merchant navy – all of which in turn stimulated industry still further, and all of which were essential prerequisites of a wartime economy.

This economic strength translated easily into military power. The German High Seas Fleet possessed 13 dreadnought battleships, compelling the British to bring their capital ships back to the North Sea. Although smaller than the Royal Navy, Germany's fleet was more modern, and boasted superior shells and night training. Her army was smaller than Russia's and only matched France's in size, but Germany could mobilise 8 million reservists and, due to superior training, deploy them at the front lines, unlike her rivals. Furthermore, Germany benefited from superior staff training, advanced technology (especially heavy artillery) and an excellent railway network, ensuring rapid mobilisation. Defence spending had increased from $204 million in 1910 to $442 million in 1914, with a compliant Reichstag's approval in 1913 of a new military budget. Germany was consequently spending more on her military than either France or Russia.

However, this military muscle bred over-confidence. The German government made very few preparations for a long war before the outbreak of hostilities. Observers, from the elder Von Moltke (commander of the Prussian army in 1870–1) to Walther Rathenau, President of AEG, had warned that future wars would be long ones, won by the economically best-equipped side. However, the Kaiser's government and generals had not grasped this, and only after 1912 did the younger Von Moltke begin to address Germany's possible wartime economic needs.

These were many, and serious problems existed. Germany possessed fine agricultural land and German farmers produced more crops per hectare than any other country, even the USA. However, because of the demands of the growing urban population, one-third of food consumed in Germany was imported, notably grain from the USA and Russia. This would prove a vital weakness in wartime, when Germany became vulnerable to blockade by Britain. The government dismissed this possibility, as they believed that Britain would not fight, and they relied upon Von Tirpitz's much-vaunted navy to prevent a blockade. Such lofty assumptions would prove fatal. Germany also imported a wide range of crucial industrial raw materials such as oil, rubber and nitrates, without which her industries would struggle in wartime. Little thought had been given before 1914 to how to obtain these products.

Germany went to war possessing only one military plan, the Schlieffen Plan. This envisaged a rapid campaign against France in the west, whilst Britain stood aside and Russia mobilised slowly. With France eliminated (in six weeks!), the German army would turn on Russia, defeating them in six months. Following this assumption, the German government had made few preparations for the kind of war they actually faced. Only with the failure of the Schlieffen Plan did Germany contemplate economic mobilisation to meet the demands of the war.

Russia had been industrialising rapidly before 1914, but it remained at a relatively early stage in its development, and war on the vast scale of 1914–18 was beyond Russia's capacity to cope. Russia had a huge population (170 million) and vast natural resources; however, she found these assets very difficult to exploit. Her population was young – 49 per cent were too young to be conscripted – and it was widely dispersed across the largest state on earth. Finally, it was deemed impossible to mobilise the millions belonging to Russia's alienated ethnic minorities, because their loyalty could not be relied upon after decades of 'russification'. An attempt in 1916 to conscript Moslems from Turkmenistan resulted in revolt.

Unlike Germany, Russia could at least feed herself. However, despite good harvests, a German blockade meant that Russia lost export markets (Germany had been Russia's biggest customer for grain, which accounted for 85 per cent of all exports), denying the state valuable income at a time when it needed to increase revenues. The financial crisis was worsened by the decision to ban the sale of vodka. Intended to make the workforce more productive, instead workers and peasants bypassed the edict by distilling their own illegal spirit. All that was achieved was to reduce the state's income by 650 million roubles per annum as it possessed a monopoly on the production and sale of vodka.

Transport was Russia's greatest headache. The Black Sea and Baltic ports were blockaded, and the only alternative routes for external trade were Vladivostock on the Pacific coast (5,000 miles away from the front line), Archangel in the North, which was ice-bound six months of the year, and Murmansk, ice-free, but which had no rail link with Moscow and Petrograd in 1914. Indeed Russia's railway network was poorly maintained, and was spread very thinly in a massive country. Germany had ten times more railways per kilometre than Russia.

Like her rivals, Russia had not anticipated the demands of a long European conflict. Between January and July 1914 Russia's biggest rifle factory, the Tula works, made only 16 rifles, due to strike action. When war broke out, the state mobilised 1.4 million men, supplying them with weapons and ammunition from existing stockpiles, but after September the situation rapidly deteriorated. State arsenals in 1914 possessed only 40 heavy guns, with 1,000 shells per gun; once these were fired, they were rationed to two per day. Only 290 million bullets were produced per year, but 200 million would be fired each month! Consequently, Russian soldiers ran short of bullets and shells by the New Year. By 1915, Russia was only producing 25 per cent of what she needed, and there were 6.5 million men under arms but only 4.6 million rifles.[3]

Yet, after the dramatic defeat by Japan in 1905, the army and navy had been substantially modernised. Defence received 33 per cent of government revenue. Russia's army numbered 1.4 million men, significantly larger than Germany's. Even Von Moltke seemed impressed, 'Russian preparedness for war has made great strides since the Russo-Japanese War.'[4] A General Staff had been created. However, the army was still dominated by the aristocracy who resented the new 'bourgeois' professional soldiers, and, consequently, there was a lack of cooperation between cavalry, infantry, artillery and navy. The Minister of War, Sukhomlinov further undermined confidence by appointing his clients to army posts in order to thwart his rival, Grand Duke Nicholas, who commanded the army. Unsurprisingly, then, the army was badly led. One observer noted that 'heavy losses resulted from unintelligent leadership and a lack of the proper equipment'.[5]

Great Britain, after her economic heyday in the mid-nineteenth century, had found her primacy challenged since 1873. Britain's share of the world's manufacturing output had declined from nearly 20 per cent in 1860 to 14 per cent by 1914. While her rate of growth in exports of manufactured goods continued to grow by 2.72 per cent per annum, Britain's industrial base was worryingly narrow, based on the same staple industries of textiles, coal, iron, shipbuilding and engineering, which had been so profitable in the previous century, yet which were now increasingly outdated in their technology. New industries such as electrical manufactures, rayon production and chemicals only contributed

6.5 per cent of all output, in contrast to the USA and Germany. For many vital industrial components, such as ball-bearings, optical glass, magnetos, dyes and drugs, Britain relied on Germany.

As an island with a vast overseas Empire, Britain had, historically, depended on her navy for protection and expansion. The army's role was to subdue those parts of the Empire which gunboats could not reach. Inevitably, the commitment to intervene on France's side on the occasion of a German attack had rendered this position redundant, but Britain's traditional dislike of large peacetime armies prevented expansion being in any way adequate. R.B. Haldane, Secretary of State for War from 1905 to 1912, had established an army general staff and a Territorial Force and prepared a British Expeditionary Force (BEF) for immediate deployment on the continent, but the army in 1914 comprised fewer than 250,000 men, scattered across the world, with reserves of 213,000. Only £29 million a year was spent on the army, compared to £51.5 million on the navy. In some ways this was understandable, as Britain imported 50 per cent of the meat, 80 per cent of the wheat and 65 per cent of the dairy products that she needed for her population of 45 million, and the navy could guarantee that Britain would be fed in the event of a global war – and it did so until the German submarines improved in range and daring.

When the conflict began, a meeting of the Army Council on 5 August, with ministers present, decided, for the first time, to send the whole of the BEF abroad, and leave the territorials at home to guard against invasion. Sir Henry Wilson, director of military operations, suggested that the BEF be sent to Maubeuge to protect the left flank of the French army. In this way the BEF 'became an auxiliary to the French army'[6] and found itself facing the full force of the German invasion. In the battles of 1914, this relatively small professional army suffered such casualties that a mass recruitment of British men and women, on a scale unknown since the Civil War, was required.

Although the same size as Germany, France possessed only 40 million people, compared to Germany's 66 million. Furthermore, the population was growing relatively slowly, at half the rate of Germany's, so, when war came, France was forced to conscript a higher proportion of her male population than her enemy.

Her standing army was comparable in size to the German army (736,000 regulars), but France had only 5 million men of conscriptable age, and could call upon only 3.5 million trained reservists, half as many as Germany. Furthermore, the army was poorly equipped. Only three weeks before war broke out, the defence expert Charles Humbert reported to a shocked Senate that France's military was wholly unready for any future war. The artillery was of poor quality, the munitions inadequate, the uniforms and boots of the soldiers inappropriate and insufficient in number. The Minister of War promised an outraged Senate that improvements would be made 'by 1917'![7]

Like the other powers, France had made few preparations for a long war. In their mobilisation plan, Plan 17, devised in 1912, the General Staff had estimated that 13,500 shells a day would be needed. It was believed that these demands could be met from existing production, and so no plans were made to increase the numbers of munitions workers, of which there were only 50,000, mostly employed in state enterprises. (The great private arms manufacturers generally exported their products, although some arms contracts were granted to the more influential manufacturers – Le Creusot for example.) Indeed, there was no reference in Plan 17 to any need to mobilise industry specially to meet the demands of a future war.

Inevitably, once war began, the state quickly realised its error. During August 1914, national production of shells was only 10,000 per day, but some individual batteries were firing 1,000 per day. Consequently, shortages rapidly occurred. This parlous situation was worsened by the fact that Germany had invaded France in August 1914, and now occupied 32,000 sq. km of industrially important northern France. In her hour of greatest need France was deprived of 81 per cent of her iron production, 74 per cent of her coal reserves, 63 per cent of her steel production, the important Kuhlmann chemicals works and 10 per cent of her population, including the important industrial city of Lille.

Consequently, in the early months of the war, production in key war industries actually fell. Coal output fell from 41 million tons (1913) to 27.5 million (1914). Iron and steel witnessed similar falls.

The war declared in August 1914 was not expected to last long. Every belligerent power had war plans, mobilisation orders and stockpiles, and the military machines that lurched into action were the mightiest that had ever been seen. However, no government had made plans to mobilise society and the economy to any great extent, and the total war in which they found themselves embroiled caught every state by surprise. Germany was superficially perhaps best equipped to deal with the rapid expansion of the war effort required from the outset. Even here, however, few advance plans had been made, and the economies of the European powers struggled to fulfil the demands of 'Total War'.

Questions

1. Which of the Great Powers' economies was best prepared to fight a sustained war?

2. Did the British navy's control of sea-borne traffic place the Germany economy at an insurmountable disadvantage?

ANALYSIS (2): HOW POLITICALLY UNIFIED WERE THE GREAT POWERS IN 1914?

Despite the post-war myth of an idyllic pre-war 'golden age', all four powers had faced serious political crises before 1914, which the euphoria of war hid in proclamations of national unity, but which were to re-emerge as the conflict wore on.

In Germany, the Bismarckian constitution, dominated by the Kaiser, the Junkers, the army and Prussia, was seen as increasingly outdated by a highly urbanised, literate population. Wilhelm II's erratic behaviour had lost the respect of many, especially after 1908 when he had unwisely given a provocative interview to the English *Daily Telegraph* without ministerial approval and his court had been rocked by rumours of the homosexuality of his closest adviser Phillip von Eulenberg. The rapid indus-trialisation of Germany since 1870 meant that the rural constituencies, dominated by the conservative landowners, were favoured by the electoral system to the detriment of the towns and cities where most Germans now lived. The army's prestige had been somewhat tarnished by the Zabern Affair of 1913 when German officers had escaped punishment following their mistreatment of civilians in an Alsatian town, though it is unwise to exaggerate the impact of this, as the army, the founder of the German state, was still held in considerable popular regard. Prussia's dominance of the constitution, wherein the Prussian regional assembly (Landtag), elected on a franchise which favoured the upper classes, could effectively veto Reichstag legislation, was the major political complaint of the powerful Social Democratic Party (SPD), which championed the cause of the industrial workers and which had become the largest party in the Reichstag in the most recent elections of 1912.

When war broke out, despite socialist anti-war demonstrations, the SPD swallowed the government's line that Germany was only acting in self-defence and joined a unanimous Reichstag vote for war-credits, despite the discomfort of some individual members such as Karl Liebknecht. This 'Burgfriede' (political truce) was, therefore, based on an interpretation of the conflict which became increasingly difficult to sustain as the war dragged on, and the suspicion grew that the 'Burgfriede' benefited the authorities far more than the workers and their political representatives.

Although the tsarist regime in Russia had granted the establishment of a Duma or parliament in 1906, its powers and influence were weak and its ability to represent the mood of the population had been undermined by Stolypin's constitutional coup in 1907, following the failure of the first two Dumas to co-operate with the government. In the years after Stolypin's death in 1911, a series of ministerial non-descripts presided over a marked upsurge in popular unrest. The massacre of protesting gold-miners at Lena in 1912 had triggered a wave of strikes, culminating in a general strike in St Petersburg in 1914. The peasantry, the bulk of the Russian population, were undergoing a period of reform, designed to encourage them to become more efficient, independent producers. In some parts of the country this set traditionalists against reformers, but it seems clear from the petitions, declarations and resolutions of peasant bodies that the reforms failed to address their key complaint, namely 'land hunger', dating back to their emancipation in 1861. The Tsar mean-while, more interested in his family and the influence of the mystic 'healer' Rasputin, toyed with the idea of abolishing the Duma and returning to openly autocratic rule.

The declaration of war in 1914, therefore, offered to unify a divided society in a defensive war, protecting fellow Slavs in Serbia from the Austrians, and themselves from the Germans. Initially, this seemed to happen. The strike movement subsided and 96 per cent of those called up for active service responded immediately. The President of the Duma, Rodzianko, told a minister, 'we shall only hinder you, it is better to dismiss us altogether until the end of hostilities',[8] while the leader of the Constitutional Democrats, Miliukov, encouraged his supporters to back the government. But it was not all patriotic enthusiasm and loyalty. When the Duma voted approval of government action and credits for the war, the five Bolshevik, six Menshevik and ten left-wing Social-Revolutionaries walked out or abstained. Outside the cities, witnesses described little joy among the peasants who would have to do the fighting. One Kadet leader noted, 'In the depths of rural Russia, eternal silence reigned.'[9] Most peasants identified themselves with their province or district and hardly at all with Russia as a whole. They saw the war as irrelevant to them, provided it didn't threaten their homes. Some conservatives foresaw difficulties as well. The Minister of the Interior wrote 'War cannot be popular among the broad masses of the people who are more receptive to the ideas of revolution than of victory over Germany.'[10] Even Rasputin talked darkly of his vision of the country bathed in blood and the end of the Romanov dynasty.

Although Britain is often perceived as the most internally unified country in Europe in 1914, recent research has begun to question this perception.[11] A serious constitutional struggle between the Liberal government in the House of Commons and the Conservative opposition in the House of Lords had led to the reduction of the powers of the latter, but the continued delay of important legislation. Daily life for Cabinet ministers was disrupted by the inventive and well-disciplined tactics of the suffragettes, whose campaign for women's rights had divided the country between opponents, unequivocal supporters and those who agreed with the cause whilst eschewing their growing militancy. The government had faced a serious wave of industrial disorder, focused in South Wales, the north of England and Clydeside, which had required the Home Secretary, Winston Churchill, to send in troops to keep order on several occasions. Most seriously of all, the Liberals' reliance on the Irish Nationalists to keep them in power after the general election of December 1910 had re-ignited the issue of Home Rule for Ireland, which the Irish demanded in return for their compliance. After the defeat of the Lords, the Protestant Ulstermen had resorted to force to defend their cause of continued Union with Britain, smuggling in guns with the tacit approval of many senior figures in the British army in Ireland. They had been encouraged by an increasingly office-hungry Conservative Party, whose leader, Andrew Bonar Law, had declared 'I can imagine no length to which Ulster will go which I shall not be ready to support',[12] thereby giving political respectability to para-military action on behalf of the Ulstermen. When the government had tried to send reinforcements to the north of Ireland, officers had resigned in protest, in the so-called 'Curragh mutiny'. Finally, having failed to stop Unionist gun-running, the army attempted unsuccessfully to prevent Nationalists landing guns at Howth, near Dublin, on 26 July 1914. This demonstration of supposed British favouritism was compounded by the troops, who then opened fire on an unarmed crowd in Dublin, killing three people. It seemed Ireland was on the verge of civil war.

However, the British government's careful handling of the declaration of war, justified by Germany's violation of 'brave little Belgium', succeeded in uniting most of the country behind it. Anti-war demonstrations, which had been huge on 3 August, quickly evaporated and floods of volunteers from all classes demonstrated the extent of national unity. Ulstermen and Irish Nationalists vied to demonstrate their commitment to the greater cause, in the hope of gaining political advantage after the war; suffragettes organised rallies demanding to serve the country; and strikes immediately ceased. There were, of course, exceptions: Ramsay MacDonald resigned as Chairman of the Parliamentary Labour Party rather than support the war; Sylvia Pankhurst finally broke with her mother Emmeline to stand against the conflict; and a group of extreme Irish Nationalists followed the example of the tiny nationalist party, Sinn Fein, almost immediately opening negotiations with the Germans for help in plotting an independence rising.

In Third Republic France, successive governments had attempted to escape the shame of defeat in 1871 by introducing universal conscription and promoting pride in the army's colonial adventures. As time had gone on, however, anti-militarism had grown, and the true divisions of French society had been laid bare by the Dreyfus affair of 1894–1906, when the army had found its most senior Jewish officer guilty of treason on the flimsiest of evidence. The division between anti-Semitic, Catholic, conservative France and the liberal, anti-clerical republicans had left scars not healed by the reprieve and reinstatement of Dreyfus, and the government feared that deeply embedded social and political divisions of pre-war France would surface upon the outbreak of war. Belle Epoque France was also riven by trade union discontent, exacerbated by governmental instability, with ten ministries since 1909. The CGT, a radical socialist union, had made no secret of its internationalist leanings and its anti-militarism, and was widely expected to organise strikes and protests in a last-ditch attempt to avert war and disrupt the call-up. Poincaré's government had even drawn up a list of prominent socialists to round up and detain in order to forestall this, the infamous Carnet B.

In the event disruption did not occur, partly because the murder of Jean Jaurès deprived the anti-war movement of its most dynamic and able leader, and partly because the Germans had so obviously aggressed against a France desperate to preserve the peace. The whole nation rallied behind their embattled motherland in a grim realisation that war was necessary, and the cry 'la patrie en danger' brought forth over 99 per cent of draftees. However, in rural France, which had just begun to gather the harvest, the news of war and the mobilisation order were greeted with anguish, alarm and consternation. The degree of determination and resolution exhibited in the early days of the war can be witnessed by the efforts of those left behind to gather the harvest and maintain food production, despite the absence of the young men.

The President of the Republic, Raymond Poincaré, called upon the nation to set aside its pre-war differences and form a 'union sacrée' against the invader. When his Socialist Prime Minister Viviani read this declaration to the National Assembly, Parliament declared its rousing support for the war, approved the request for a state of siege to be declared, and adjourned, allowing the government rule by decree 'for the duration of the crisis'. Viviani promptly formed a new bi-partisan government, enlisting opposition notables like Briand and Delcassé, and even drafting in three radical socialists. A 'Comité de Secours National' was formed which included the Archbishop of Paris, the Secretary of the Confederation General de Travail, the Paris Préfet de Police and the leader of the extreme right-wing group Action Française.

Whilst Becker's observation that 'it is no longer possible to claim that France was swept by a wave of enthusiasm' is valid, it remains true that, despite the initial shock and sadness at the onset of war, France quickly united behind the 'union sacrée'. The government's fears of anti-war demonstrations by the stridently pacifistic French union movement proved groundless, and the nation, in the words of one cynical observer, 'began settling down to war'.

It is, of course, a fruitless task to attempt to discern which of the European powers was the most politically united, but it needs to be noted that Russia's severe economic and military weakness on top of the political gulf between rulers and people must single her out as the power least likely to maintain the political will to fight a war she was unprepared for. The other countries each possessed strengths and weaknesses, but it was clear that a long and punishing war would test the commitment of the German people to a regime that they had already begun to criticise, while the British would face continued worries over Ireland's stability. Industrially backward France, as long as she had another ally to fight with, had the determination, following her defeat in 1871, and the incentive, with the enemy occupying French soil, to fight to the extreme limits of her endurance. Much would depend on the duration of the war and the burdens it placed on the population as a whole.

Questions

1. How far was the extent of social unity determined by the degree of popular participation in the governments of the Great Powers?
2. Did the governments of 1914 actively seek war for political advantage?

SOURCES

1. THE ECONOMIES OF THE GREAT POWERS

Source A: German industrial employment (1907).

Size of firm (no of employees)	No. of industrial firms	Total no. of employees
11–50	89,645	1,985,295
51–200	23,493	2,176,053
201–1,000	4,993	1,875,628
Over 1,000	478	879,305

Source B: French industrial employment (1906).

Size of firm (no. of employees)	Percentage of total
Less than 10	59%
11–100	16%
More than 100	25%

Source C: railways as indicators of economic strength (1910 figures).

	(i) km railway	(ii) km railway/km area
Germany	61,000 km	12
Britain	38,000 km	12
France	49,500 km	10
Russia	70,000 km	1

Source D: foreign trade in 1913 (valued in £ millions).

Russia	190	France	424
Germany	1,030	Britain	1,223

Source E: comparative growth in national income (GDP) 1894–1913.

Britain	70%	Germany	58%
European Russia	50%	France	52%

Source F: output in key industries in 1913 (measured in millions of tons).

	Coal	Iron	Steel
Germany	190	16.7	17.5
France	40	5.2	4.6
Russia	35	4.6	4.8
Britain	292	10.4	7.7

Source G: two estimates of the population of major European states in 1913.

(i)

Country	Population
France	39.6 million
Germany	64.9 million
Russia	160.7 million
United Kingdom	40.8 million

(ii)

Country	Population
France	39.7 million
Germany	66.9 million
Russia	175.1 million
United Kingdom	45.6 million

Source H: Paul Kennedy, a modern historian, comments on the state of Russia in 1914.

Russia in the decades prior to 1914 was simultaneously powerful and weak – depending as ever upon which end of the telescope one peered down.... It was much stronger industrially than at the time of the Crimean War. Between 1860 and 1913 – a very lengthy period – Russian industrial output grew at the impressive annual average rate of 5 per cent.... Its steel production on the eve of the first world war had overtaken France's and Austria-Hungary's.... Its coal output was rising even faster.... Enormous factories, frequently employing thousands of workers, sprang up around St Petersburg, Moscow and other major cities.... By 1914, as many historians have pointed out, Russia had become the fourth industrial power in the world....

A look through the telescope from the other end, however, produces a quite different picture. Even if there were approximately 3 million workers in Russian factories by 1914, that represented the appallingly low level of 1.75 per cent of the population.... What was perhaps even more significant was the extent to which Russian industrialisation, despite some indigenous entrepreneurs, was carried out by foreigners ... or had at least been created by foreign investors. 'By 1914, 90 per cent of mining, almost 100 per cent of oil extraction, 40 per cent of the metallurgical industry, 50 per cent of the chemical industry and even 28 per cent of the textile industry were foreign owned.' ... By the early 20th century Russia had incurred the largest foreign debt in the world.

Questions

1. Explain why column (i) in Source C would be misleading without the addition of column (ii). (3 marks)
*2. Compare Sources A and B. What do they tell us about French and German industry before World War One? (4 marks)
3. How does Source G illustrate the difficulties inherent in any

assessment of the relative strength of the powers in 1914? (4 marks)

4. How far do Sources C to F support the judgement of Paul Kennedy (Source H) regarding the state of Russia in 1914? (6 marks)

5. How far do the Sources provided, and your own knowledge, support the view that Germany, of all the European powers, ought to have been ready for a large war in 1914? (8 marks)

Worked answer

2. [Comparative questions usually require you to identify both similarities and differences between the sources under scrutiny. If you are asked to compare tables of statistics, as in this question, you also need to consider the limitations of the information that is presented to you.]

Sources A and B address the size of industrial firms around 1906, and reveal that German industry was organised on a larger scale than in France. From these sources, it appears that, whilst French industrial firms were mostly very small workshop-based enterprises, with fewer than 11 employees, German industrial organisation was on a larger scale. On the basis of the figures given in Source A, we see that most German firms employed between 11 and 200 workers (this accounts for 94 per cent of the total number of firms given here).

However, Source B only gives us a percentage of the whole, and not the raw data. Thus we do not know how many French firms we are discussing. Meanwhile, Source A leaves out firms with fewer than ten employees, and we are unable to compare what proportion of German firms there were employing fewer than ten employees with the French figure. Thus, we are unable to compare the two sets of figures directly, and are forced to make conditional judgements, based on incompatible statistical data, which is unsatisfactory.

SOURCES

2. POLITICAL UNITY AMONG THE GREAT POWERS IN 1914

Source I: from Wilhelm II's speech from the balcony of the Royal Palace, Berlin, 1 August 1914.

I thank you from the bottom of my heart for the expression of your loyalty and your esteem. When it comes to war, all parties cease and we are all brothers.

One or another party has attacked me in peacetime, but now I forgive them wholeheartedly. If our neighbours do not give us peace, then we hope and wish that our good German sword will come victorious out of this war!

Source J: from a speech by Friedrich Ebert (leader of SPD) to the Reichstag, August 1914.

Everything is at stake for our nation and its development towards liberty in the future if Russian despotism stained with the best blood of its people should be victorious.

It is our duty to ward off this danger, to protect the civilisation (*Kultur*) and independence of our own country. Thus we carry out what we have always emphasised: In the hour of danger we shall not desert the Fatherland. In saying this we feel ourselves in accord with the International which has always recognised the right of every nation to national independence and self-defence, just as we agree with it in condemning any war of aggression or conquest.

We hope that the cruel experience of suffering in this war will awaken in many millions of people the abhorrence of war and will win them for the ideals of socialism and world peace.

We demand that as soon as the aim of security has been achieved and our opponents are disposed to make peace this war shall be brought to an end by treaty of peace which makes friendship possible with our neighbours. We ask this not only in the interest of national solidarity for which we have always contended, but also in the interest of the German people.

With these principles in mind, we vote the desired war credits.

Source K: from Sir Edward Grey's speech before Parliament, 3 August 1914.

If France is beaten in a struggle of life and death, beaten to her knees, loses her position as a great power, becomes subordinate to the will and power of one greater than herself, consequences which I do not anticipate, because I am sure that France has the power to defend herself with all the energy and ability and patriotism which she has shown so often [Loud cheers.] – still, if that were to happen and if Belgium fell under the same dominating influence, and then Holland, and then Denmark, then would not Mr. Gladstone's words come true, that just opposite to us there would be a common interest against the unmeasured aggrandisement of any power? [Loud cheers.]

It may be said, I suppose, that we might stand aside, husband our strength, and that, whatever happened in the course of this war, at the end of it intervene with effect to put things right, and to adjust them to our own point of view. If, in a crisis like this, we run away [Loud cheers.] from those obligations of honour and interest as regards the Belgian treaty, I doubt whether, whatever material force we might have at the end, it would be of very much value in face of the respect that we should have lost. And I do not believe, whether a great power stands outside this war or not, it is going to be in a position at the end of it to exert its superior strength. For us, with a powerful fleet, which we believe able to protect our commerce, to protect our shores, and to protect our interests, if we are engaged in war, we shall suffer but little more than we shall suffer even if we stand aside.

Source L: from President Poincaré's War Message, 4 August 1914.

At the hour when the struggle is beginning, France has the right, in justice to herself, of solemnly declaring that she has made, up to the last moment, supreme efforts to avert the war now about to break out, the crushing responsibility for which the German Empire will have to bear before history. [Unanimous and repeated applause.] Our fine and courageous army, which France today accompanies with her maternal thought [loud applause] has risen eager to defend the honour of the flag and the soil of the country. [Unanimous and repeated applause.]

In the war which is beginning, France will have Right on her side, the eternal power of which cannot with impunity be disregarded by nations any more than by individuals [loud and unanimous applause].

She will be heroically defended by all her sons; nothing will break their sacred union before the enemy; today they are joined together as brothers in a common indignation against the aggressor, and in a common patriotic faith [loud and prolonged applause and cries of 'Vive la France'].

Source M: from the Moscow declaration of zemstvo representatives, 25 July 1914.

Gone are now the barriers which have divided our citizens; all are united in one common effort ... who, if not the members of public institutions whose business it is to provide for the needs of the people, who have had many years of practical experience in caring for the sick, and who have organised forces at their command, should undertake the task of uniting isolated efforts in their great work, which demands so immense an organisation.

Questions

1. (i) Explain the reference to 'the International' (Source J). (2 marks)
   (ii) Explain the reference to 'the Belgian treaty' (Source K). (2 marks)
2. What is the main difference between Sources I and J in their support for German unity in the face of war? (4 marks)

3. Compare the justifications each national representative gives for the declaration of war in Sources J, K and L. (6 marks)
4. What is the purpose of the declaration of zemstvo representatives (Source M)? (3 marks)
*5. In light of your own knowledge, how far do the Sources reveal German and Russian support for the war to be less wholehearted than in Britain and France? (8 marks)

Worked answer

*5. *[This question carries the most marks and should therefore produce the longest answer. Although it is the last question asked, you must ensure that you have sufficient time left to answer it. As you have to consider the reaction to the war in four countries, it would be advisable to analyse Russia and Germany separately from Britain and France as the question suggests. You must ensure that you refer to all the sources, preferably identifying them by letter, and clearly display your own knowledge as well.]*

In Sources I, J and M, all those declaring their support for national unity in the face of war, do so with reservations. The Kaiser, in Source I, cannot resist mentioning those who 'attacked me in peacetime', meaning the Social Democrats, the Centre Party and even Conservatives such as von Bülow. In this way, he is laying bare the lack of pre-war political unity and unconsciously distinguishing between support for him and support for the German national war effort. This theme is continued in source J, where Ebert makes the pledge, 'we shall not desert the Fatherland', not mentioning support for the government or the Kaiser. In fact, he goes on to express the hope that the war will advance the cause of socialism, the very threat that the German government had hoped to avoid by going to war. More importantly, Ebert only pledges support for a war to ensure German security. While the German High Command and government could argue that such security was only possible with the defeat of the Allies, the so-called 'September Programme' of 1914 soon revealed that the elite forces of Germany had plans to annex vast areas of Eastern Europe once victory was achieved. As the war continued, therefore, the support of the SPD became increasingly fragile, as they insisted on a 'peace without annexations and indemnities'. In Source M, the zemstva representatives, although not placing conditions on their support, make it clear that they believe that they can contribute much to the war effort, due to their experience in local government. It could be said that the comment that the war 'demands so immense an organisation' is an implied rebuff for the government, whose administrative incompetence was well known. The zemstvo representatives knew that Russian officials closely guarded their power and are trying to use the opportunity of the war to their political advantage by gaining greater access to civil administration.

For Britain and France, however, the sources reveal a much clearer sense of purpose and national involvement. In Source K, Sir Edward Grey effectively combines the demands of honour, in defending 'the Belgian treaty' of 1839 which guaranteed Belgian neutrality, and the traditional pragmatism of British foreign policy, which was designed to prevent 'the unmeasured aggrandisement of any power' on the continent. It could be said that Grey's speech fails to reconcile the British policy of defending one small nation, Belgium, whilst continuing to impose her will on a very reluctant Ireland, but such views were only held by extremist Nationalists in 1914. In the case of France, Poincaré is able to honestly portray her as the injured party, and to appeal to the patriotism of his people to defend the country against an aggressor who has, within living memory, invaded before. The statement in source L that 'France will have Right on her side' effectively summarises the position of the majority of French opinion, especially since the most effective anti-war politician, Jean Jaurès, had recently been silenced by a right-wing assassin's bullet.

2

RECRUITMENT AND PROPAGANDA

BACKGROUND NARRATIVE

The initial months of the war were in fact the most decisive. The Germans failed to destroy the French army, faced with unexpected Belgian resistance and a French and British retreat, which prevented the Allies suffering the fate of encirclement which had befallen the French in 1870. Instead the Allies fought back at the Marne and pushed the Germans back to a line 50 miles from the French capital. There the Germans dug in, deciding to wait for the Allies to bring the war to them, as the current military technology of machine gun, barbed wire and heavy artillery favoured a defensive approach. Meanwhile the unexpectedly swift invasion of East Prussia by the Russians had diverted two German divisions from the west at a vital moment, but left the Russian forces divided and over-stretched. General Hindenburg was brought out of retirement and, with his able quarter-master general, Eric Ludendorff, managed to inflict crushing defeats on the two Russian armies in East Prussia at Tannenberg and the Masurian Lakes. The Germans swiftly advanced into Russian Poland, but any further advances were halted by the onset of winter. The Russians had more success in the south against the Austrian army, invading the Austro-Hungarian Empire, but the war had cost hundreds of thousands of Russian casualties before Christmas 1914.

For all the powers, as hopes of swift victory were dashed, realisation grew that in this war victory depended on more than the physical bravery of the soldiers. The ability to replace losses and supply armies with all the resources they needed to keep fighting, both high-technology weapons and basic necessities, would determine a nation's chances of victory in a large-scale, long-duration war. The governments of Europe therefore turned, with varying degrees of urgency, to the task of involving the whole of their population in the war effort and convincing them that the sacrifices and commitment required were justified by the cause in which they served.

Military authorities were, inevitably, cautious in revealing information which may have been of help to the enemy, but most censorship was actually self-imposed by the press. During September 1914, French newspapers failed to accurately report the colossal scale of French losses. In the following month, the loss of the British battleship *Audacious* was not mentioned, despite the wreck being seen by passenger liners on their way to America. Most notoriously, newspapers reported that soldiers viewed war with enthusiasm and were disdainful of its dangers. In France, where war was seen as unwanted, but unavoidable, propagandists emphasised the soldiers' alleged patriotism and gaiety in the face of death. A correspondent told readers of *Le Petit Parisien* that 'our troops laugh at the machine guns now. . . . Nobody pays the slightest attention to them', while *Echo de Paris* reported the story of one wounded soldier: 'My wound? It doesn't matter. . . . But make sure you tell them that all Germans are cowards and that the only problem is how to get at them.' Stories of soldiers kicking footballs towards the enemy and looking forward to a 'scrap' continued throughout the war, and, in the accounts of soldiers, did more to distance the realities of life on the front line from the patriots on the Home Front.

The most famous propaganda technique employed in the First World War, which all governments and most journalists used, was that of the atrocity story. In Britain especially, where there was a need after 1914 to keep up the flow of volunteers, such stories flourished. One of the earliest stories, that of Grace Hume, a 23-year-old nurse, appeared in the *Evening Standard*, *Pall Gazette*, *Westminster Gazette* and *The Star* in September 1914. The report described how invading German soldiers at Vilvorde in Belgium had attacked a camp hospital, killing wounded soldiers, and then cut off Nurse Hume's breast. *The Times*, however, discovered that Nurse Hume was actually in Huddersfield and had never been to Belgium, the whole story being fabricated by Grace Hume's younger sister, Kate, who was charged with forgery and convicted. None of the newspapers which had printed the original story printed a retraction.[1]

ANALYSIS (1): HOW EFFECTIVELY DID THE GREAT POWERS MOBILISE THEIR PEOPLE FOR WAR?

All the Great Powers had plans to mobilise their forces for war and these were put into effect as the crisis escalated in late July 1914. Germany was placed under martial law on 31 July as the Siege Law of 1871 was invoked, and 24 army districts were created, headed by generals, who 'wielded an almost unlimited power in the case of civil administration and political rights generally, as well as in military matters'.[2] Bridges, viaducts, rail terminals and road junctions were guarded by militia. Trains were seized, returning holidaymakers and their luggage dumped off, and German troops packed in, issued with iron rations, 90 rounds of ammunition, a songbook and a prayer book. Every day 550 troop trains crossed the Rhine, decorated with signs saying 'To Paris' and 'To London'. The enormous scale of mobilisation meant that Germany suffered a massive dislocation to her infrastructure. The most productive part of the workforce had been mobilised and many small businesses were forced to close, sending unemployment rocketing. As the army monopolised transport, companies were unable to get supplies and to fulfil orders. The electrical company Siemens lost foreign orders for 5.8 million light bulbs in this way.[3] As early as August, Berlin trams were operated by women, and a nationwide campaign was begun for towns-people (including schoolchildren) to gather in the harvest, with free rail tickets issued to get them to the farms. Expecting a short war, the War Ministry had not, however, planned how to distribute manpower between the front line and the factory, and the munitions crisis which befell Germany in autumn 1914 created an immediate labour crisis.

It was Russian mobilisation, begun on 31 July, that triggered this frenzied activity on the German part, for the German plan of attack, the Schlieffen Plan, required Germany to attack and defeat France before the massive Russian army could attack her. Since 1910, however, Russia had been improving her rail links with the West and had been increasing the amount of rolling stock available. Whereas Schlieffen's plan had anticipated that fewer than 200 trains would be available for mobilisation per day, by 1914 that figure had increased to 360. When Russia mobilised, using her war plan, No. 19 (amended), she had 208 battalions of infantry and 228 squadrons of cavalry organised in the I and II armies by 11 August, facing less then 100 battalions of the German VIII army in East Prussia. The Russian army crossed the German border on 15 August and engaged German troops almost immediately. They may have been unprepared for the nature of the fighting to come, but Russia's swift mobilisation had destroyed any possibility of the Schlieffen Plan working to order, as German troops had to be diverted from the advance on Paris in the west to drive the Russians off German soil.

Russian mobilisation also involved the handing-over of authority over territories in the front line and military installations elsewhere, to the army command. In the areas they controlled, the command did not need to consult civilian authorities, and could dismiss any officials, including governors and chairmen of the local government boards (zemstvo). In this way, the Russian Empire was split, between those areas controlled by Grand Duke Nikolai Nikolaevich – Poland; Finland; the Baltic; Archangel; the Caucasus; Vladivostock and Petrograd itself – and the rest of Russia, administered by Prime Minister Goremykin. This was to prove disastrous in co-ordinating supplies, especially for the cities, where reserve troops and refugees from the front line swiftly built up. There was also a complex system of exemptions and deferments which exacerbated the problems which the inadequate tsarist bureaucracy had in enforcing conscription across such a massive Empire. As a result, while France mobilised 168 of every 1,000 men for active military service, the Germans managed 154 and even Britain mustered 125, it is estimated that Russia only mobilised 5.[4]

As reserves were called up in France, Germany and Russia, and volunteers were called for in Britain, men, often highly skilled, were removed from production. Obviously, some workers were not as essential as in peacetime: luxury goods, public services and bureaucracies could all manage with less labour. As the manpower drain went on, however, the essential productivity of wartime – raw materials, food production and above all munitions – began to suffer. In France, armaments workers were given an exemption from armed service as early as September 1914, but even that was too late (Le Creusot lost 50 per cent of their workforce within days of war breaking out), as many were already in uniform and a considerable proportion were dead or wounded, as France had lost 855,000 men by the end of November 1914. Germany followed France's example and began to comb out skilled workers from the services and return them to the factories. By 1915, however, Albert Thomas, French Under-Secretary of State for Artillery and Munitions, had sided with the army in denying the industrialists' requests for more service releases. Instead he urged the arms industry to employ auxiliary workers.

By November 1918, alongside 497,000 men of military age in the arms industry, there were 430,000 women, 133,000 children, 108,000 foreigners, 61,000 colonials, 13,000 disabled workers and 40,000 prisoners of war. In this way, France was able to keep a massive army in the field as well as remaining the largest Allied producer of arms.

The need for labour in wartime also gave unions a valuable bargaining tool in their negotiations with governments. In Britain and Germany laws were passed to prevent workers changing jobs. In the case of Germany, the Patriotic Auxiliary Service Law of 1916 gave the government more control over their workforce than in any other country. All males aged between 18 and 60 had to accept essential war jobs, if they were not already on military service. Universities were closed, Sunday holidays abolished and women initially encouraged to join the workforce. When the British government passed the Munitions of War Act in 1915, strikes and stoppages were banned and compulsory arbitration was introduced to resolve disputes. The government also took direct control of certain factories concerned with war production, and in these factories all trade union rights were suspended, albeit only for the duration of the war, and wage levels were guaranteed.

Conscription and the threat of conscription were used to rid workplaces of troublesome elements by all the governments, but this sanction tended to cause class tension and was sometimes the trigger for the strikes which all the Great Powers experienced as the war went on.

In Britain, despite the challenge of the German attack and the limited size of the BEF, Parliament ruled out conscription. The army was given permission to increase in size by 500,000, but these would be volunteers. Therefore, in Britain, unlike the rest of Europe, a recruitment drive was begun, with 100,000 young men volunteering in September, as the news of the retreat from Mons began to filter through. Although, by January 1915, there were 1,342,647 recruits, the numbers of new volunteers had dwindled to fewer than 22,000 per week. With the battles of 1915 killing and maiming troops at a horrendous rate, the Parliamentary Recruiting Committee began to try new tactics, shaming potential recruits into joining up by aiming posters at women inciting them to send their men to the front. These included the famous 'Daddy, what did you do in the Great War?' poster, which prompted the Scottish miners' leader Bob Smillie to reply, 'I tried to stop the bloody thing, my child.'[5]

The Conservative Party, many of whose members also belonged to the National Service League, which called for conscription long before the war, began to demand that voluntarism be replaced by compulsion. *The Times* claimed on 6 May 1915 that 'The voluntary system has its limits and we are fast approaching them.'[6] It was clear that not only was the number of recruits decreasing, but that the propaganda campaigns were recruiting men from essential wartime production, thus inhibiting the potential size of the army by reducing the supplies that were needed to sustain it.[7] Conscription would not only guarantee the supply of men to the Front, but it could, if managed effectively, guarantee the supply of equipment to enable the British army to outlast the blockaded Germans. When Conservative ministers in Asquith's new coalition government threatened resignation, the Prime Minister produced a compromise, first introducing a National Register, which obliged every British subject aged between 16 and 65 to register for national service, and second, allowing Lord Derby's scheme to encourage men between 18 and 41 to 'attest' a willingness to serve when called upon, thus avoiding conscription. While 1.35 million married men attested, on the understanding that the unmarried would be called up first, as Asquith had promised, only 840,000 unmarried men out of a possible 2.2 million of military age did so. Asquith therefore could say that he had tried to prevent conscription, but that he had been faced with no alternative, and thus avoid the mass resignation of Liberal anti-conscriptionists that had been threatened. In the event, when Asquith introduced the Military Service Act of January 1916, which imposed conscription on single men aged between 18 and 41, with exemptions for ministers of religion, the medically unfit, the Irish and conscientious objectors, only the Home Secretary, Sir John Simon, resigned from the government in protest. It was left to local tribunals to decide which workers were carrying out 'essential' work and were also exempt, which caused a lack of consistency from one area to another and a shortage of men which was only remedied in April 1916, when conscription was extended to married men. The army and the War Office continued to complain of manpower shortages, however, even after conscription, and a War Priorities Committee was only set up late in 1917, to co-ordinate manpower needs. Yet the British army was able to help to keep the Germans at bay for four years and to act as the decisive force in bringing victory in 1918. As Gerald de Groot has written, 'In the end Britain found just enough men to squeak through to victory.'[8]

Questions

1. How far did initial mobilisation damage the economies of the Great Powers?
2. Why was France able to mobilise her manpower more successfully than the other Great Powers?

ANALYSIS (2): HOW SUCCESSFULLY DID THE GOVERNMENTS OF THE GREAT POWERS CONTROL PUBLIC OPINION DURING THE FIRST WORLD WAR?

Civilians were involved in the war effort on a previously unheard of scale, so governments needed to inspire and channel their efforts through propaganda. Most newspaper editors and journalists were quite prepared to abandon the objective perspective of the press to help them in this task. In perhaps the most dramatic example of this, the anti-establishment German magazine *Simplicissimus* decided that 'precisely now, Germany needed a journal that was internationally so respected as *Simplicissimus* to support the war effort at home and abroad' and so fell into line behind the government.[9] Similarly, the *Hamburger Fremdenblatt*, a progressive-liberal paper, became so fervently militaristic, that it criticised the 1917 Reichstag peace resolution for defeatism. The Burgfrieden was accepted by the press as well as the parties, but newspapers remained the mouthpieces of separate interest groups, rather than the country as a whole. Rather than creating a ministry of propaganda, the government allowed the military to set up their own 'German War News' service, which kept the middle-class, often Jewish, newspaper barons separate from official reports. In this way, the pre-war class divisions between the elitist army-dominated government and the people were sustained in the organisation of German propaganda.

Censors often intervened to alter or remove stories which were felt to be prejudicial to the war effort. These could often be incredibly trivial, but certain stories were inevitably more likely than others to receive attention from the official censor: for example, the Stockholm peace conference, the International socialist conferences in London and Kienthal, the peace feelers put out by Bethmann-Hollweg, Wilson and the Pope, the mutinies of 1917 and, of course, the full extent of casualties. Lists of the dead, initially published in the press to create a sense of sacrifice and outrage, were quickly suppressed, as damaging to morale. Interestingly, the French government did try to rein in some of the more ridiculous and terrifying tales of German 'barbarism', which it was felt undermined morale. Noticeably, attacks on the government were also made a target of the censor, although with rather mixed results. Governments were seeking not simply to restrict the publication of unwelcome news, but to foster 'ideas and sentiments likely to contribute to a final victory'.[10]

However, the French government was loath to completely control the press. Furthermore, the professionalism of the central agencies responsible for censorship was not matched by those at local level. Consequently, dissenting opinion was heard. This took various forms, ranging from anti-war defeatism to criticism of the specific actions of specific generals or politicians. The radical paper, *Le Crapouillet*, publicly challenged the view, peddled by the military in 1917, that the front-line mutinies resulted from the pacifist propaganda of the left-wing press, arguing controversially (but correctly) that 'most of the mutinies amongst Front Line regiments have been the inevitable result of the continual bloody and stupidly-conceived offensives'.[11] That this article made it into print suggests that censorship was not total and indiscriminate.

However, the governments of Europe quickly found that, in reality, there was little need for censorship. The press in every nation 'self-mobilised', running outrageously patriotic stories, often wholly fabricated, although this was partly because they were given so little official news with which to fill their pages. In France, a Press Commission was created, incorporating representative editors of the various press associations, to co-ordinate the distribution of war-related news. The press adopted an almost uniformly bellicose tone throughout the conflict, lauding the heroism of their troops, celebrating the victories of their generals (even when these were singularly difficult to unearth), and demonising the enemy.

The German army's undeniably harsh treatment of Belgian civilians, 5,000 of whom were executed during the war as hostages or as suspected snipers, led to the appearance of unchecked stories of mutilated children, looting and rape during the opening months of the war. Lord Northcliffe offered £200 for a genuine photograph, but the prize was never claimed. German newspapers replied in kind, printing stories of Belgian civilians mutilating wounded German soldiers, priests sniping from behind their altars, and the widespread Allied use of dumdum bullets. The British government set up the Secret War Propaganda Bureau in September 1914 to counter such German stories and to gain neutral support for the Allied cause. But apart from this they relied on the efforts of the press until 1917.

For the rest of the war, German atrocity stories continued, fed by such incidents as the execution of Nurse Edith Cavell, the sinking of the *Lusitania*, German naval and air attacks on British towns, and the first use of poisoned gas on the Western Front. When material was short, the press demonstrated an inventive approach to newsgathering, most notably in the case of the German 'corpse factory'. In 1917, *The Times*, which had exposed the fabrication of the Nurse Hume story in 1914, published a series of reports, claiming that eyewitnesses had seen the bodies of German soldiers, wrapped in barbed wire, being rendered down for fats and oils. In fact, the German word *Kadaver* had simply been translated as 'corpse' rather than the truthful meaning of 'carcass', and a rather dull German newspaper article had provided further proof of the Germans' inhumane behaviour.[12]

The lack of verification for the atrocity stories in the first months of the war led to the British government setting up a committee to investigate alleged German atrocities, under Lord Bryce, former British ambassador to Washington, consisting of lawyers and historians. The committee's report was published a few days after the sinking of the *Lusitania* and included graphic accounts of German brutality on Belgians. In this way, atrocity stories were given official confirmation, and many shared the attitude of the British ambassador in Paris, who said in May 1915, 'I began by not believing in German atrocities, and now I feel that I myself, would, if I could, kill every combatant German that I might meet.' The Secret War Propaganda Bureau sent representatives to the USA to capitalise on the timing of the report. However, no witnesses to the committee had been required to testify under oath and none were identified in the final report. The report itself included hearsay evidence, and the committee had not visited the site of the alleged atrocities. Despite a pledge to keep copies of all witness depositions at the Home Office, none have ever been found. It is ironic that the Allies did not use the genuine atrocities committed by the Turks against the Armenian population in 1915 as effectively as they did the unproven stories of massacre in Belgium.

In Russia patriotism was redefined as the war progressed, so as to separate the Tsar and the homeland. At first there was considerable self-mobilisation. The state's relatively small-scale efforts at propaganda were reinforced extensively by the contributions of artists, entertainers, writers and their patrons. The Skobelev Committee, a semi-official propaganda organisation, issued photographic postcards and had a monopoly on the production of documentary films at the front. The postcards were conservative and unimaginative and the (usually staged) newsreels were so few and inadequate that, despite the scarcity of imports, Russian movie audiences had a better picture of action on the Western Front than the Eastern Front. The Skobelev Committee operated on a commercial basis, so one may therefore assume that, as far as censorship permitted, this material sought to reflect public demand. This in turn only reflected the widespread support and sympathy for the war which society as a whole exhibited. The form which such outpourings took initially reflected traditional styles and genres, but gradually newer media were exploited, especially cinema. Images of Alexsandr Nevskii (medieval victor over the Germans), Mikhail Kutzov (Napoleonic War hero) and St George, as well as the obvious multitude of tsarist motifs and images, abounded. Noticeably, the boom in patriotic culture was confined largely to the cities. The isolated and inaccessible rural areas, with their predominantly illiterate population, were relatively untouched, especially by the newer forms that it took.

As the war went on, and the suffering of Russia intensified, 'expressions of patriotism, however, dwindled'.[13] Russia suffered from the lack of a really effective, widely accepted national symbolic figure – a John Bull or Uncle Sam. The Tsar's failure to assume this sort of role was a factor in his ultimate demise. The decline in 'Kaiser-bashing' may not have been entirely spontaneous, for in mid-1915 the nervous government banned ridicule of all crowned heads. Instead, high society sought refuge in decadent displays of luxury and opulence; the less fortunate fled into escapist cinema, preferring such films to uplifting patriotic ones. Jingoistic, triumphalist themes in tableaux and pantomimes were replaced with sentimental depictions of nurses tending the wounded, and celebrations of the simple courage of the Russian soldier, especially the Cossack. Clowns, traditionally critics of authority in Russia, and *estrada* (variety theatre) performers soon diverted their attacks from the Germans to war profiteers, some of whom might be sitting in the front rows. It was not so difficult to get from here to the anti-tsarist polemics of February 1917. Even when victory could be thought probable, these Russian media put forward little notion of anything to be gained by it. When victory ceased to be probable, patriotism did not cease to exist, but it took on a variety of meanings that helped to divide society and to weaken the state. The intellectual and moral ground was unconsciously being prepared for revolution.

After the war, German nationalists used British propaganda as an excuse for the defeat of the supposedly invincible German Imperial Army. Ludendorff himself wrote that, 'we were hypnotised by Allied propaganda, as a rabbit is by a snake. It was exceptionally clever and conceived on a grand scale.' Such an argument was also used by Hitler to justify the unparalleled degree of news management that sustained the Third Reich. What they both failed to acknowledge was that propaganda in itself was useless unless the vast majority of people were prepared to listen to and believe in it. British and French propaganda, even in its excesses of atrocity invention, proclaimed the merits of a fundamentally united people, who already believed in the rightness of the cause in which they fought. German propaganda, with its posters, films, pamphlets, poetry and songs, differed little in form from British and French efforts, but was very different in tone. The use of elitist figures, such as the 93 German intellectuals or the military authorities, to deliver the message of Germany's cause, failed to address the concerns of the working man and the non-Prussian, who, just like their counterparts in Russia, increasingly saw the war as being fought for the benefit of the upper classes. As Winter has put it, 'Hungry families needed food, not more propaganda appeals.'[14] However, one should not over-estimate the success of British and French propaganda in hiding the divisions in those countries. In Britain, when the voluntary National Service Scheme was launched in February 1917 with a huge budget for advertising, less than half the expected numbers enrolled, demonstrating the shift in popular attitudes to patriotic appeals as the war continued. In France, popular disenchantment with the blandly optimistic propaganda produced by the established press was expressed by the success of smaller, independent papers, such as Clemenceau's *Canard Enchaîné*, which took a more critical line.[15] But in both countries, this reflected a more mature popular attitude towards war reporting, rather than a rejection of the entire war effort. In both countries, it must also be said, the reliance on voluntary bodies made it impossible for the government to control the direction of propaganda. Even when both governments did intervene, they failed to establish an effective machinery of propaganda, with, for example, the British Ministry of Information set up in 1917, under Beaverbrook, often contradicting and overlapping the work of other departments, such as the Foreign Office, the Admiralty and the War Office. If propaganda did work in Britain and France, it was because it reinforced the belief in a 'just war' that both countries, on the whole, embraced.

Questions

1. To what extent were the propaganda techniques used by all the Great Powers similar?
2. Was propaganda best devised by those most closely in touch with public opinion?

SOURCES

1. MOBILISATION

Source A: from an extract by the German military attaché in St Petersburg, 26 July 1914, describing a conversation with the Russian Minister of War, Sukhomlinov.

Upon my inquiry as to the object of the mobilisation against Austria, he shrugged his shoulders and indicated the diplomats ... I got the impression of great nervousness and anxiety. I consider the wish for peace genuine, military statements in so far correct, that complete mobilisation has probably not been ordered but preparatory measures are very far reaching. They are evidently striving to gain time for new negotiations and for continuing their armaments. Also the internal situation is unmistakably causing serious anxiety.

Source B: from the records of the Russian foreign ministry, 29 July 1914.

After examining the situation from all points, both the Ministers [i.e. Sazonov and Sukhomlinov] and the Chief of the General Staff decided that in view of the small probability of avoiding a war with Germany, it was indispensable to prepare for it in every way in good time, and that therefore the risk could not be accepted of delaying a general mobilisation later by effecting a partial mobilisation now. The conclusion reached at this conference was at once reported by telephone to the Tsar, who authorised the taking of steps accordingly. The information was received with enthusiasm by the small circle of those acquainted with what was in progress.

Source C: British recruitment advertisement: to the women of London.

Is your 'Best Boy' wearing Khaki? If not, don't YOU THINK he should be?

If he does not think that you and your country are worth fighting for – do you think he is *worthy* of you?

Don't pity the girl who is alone – her young man is probably a soldier fighting for her and her country – and for YOU

If your young man neglects his duty to his King and Country, the time may come when he will NEGLECT YOU

Think it over – and then ask him to

JOIN THE ARMY – TODAY

Source D: British Prime Minister Asquith considers the future of the Derby scheme in the House of Commons, 2 November 1915.

If there should still be found a substantial number of men of military age not required for other purposes, and who, without excuse, hold back from the service of their country, I believe that the very same conditions which make compulsion impossible now – namely the absence of general consent – would force the country to a view that they must consent to supplement, by some form of legal obligation, the failure of the voluntary system.

Source E: Albert Thomas, Under-Secretary of State for Artillery and Munitions at a meeting of arms manufacturers, January 1916.

General Headquarters asks that no more men be released from service at the front, because the efforts of the commander in chief and the Ministry of War to provide the army with all men capable of military service would be compromised if the ranks of our combatants were further thinned by new requests for industrial labour. Accordingly, men will only be released from the front in cases of urgent need.

Source F: from the German Auxiliary Service Law of 5 December 1916.

I. Every male German between the ages of seventeen and sixty who is not serving in the armed forces is obligated to perform Patriotic Auxiliary Service during the war.

IX. No one may take into his employ a man liable to Patriotic Auxiliary Service who is employed or has been employed during the previous two weeks unless the applicant produces a certificate from his late employer that he has agreed to the man's leaving his service.

XII. It is the duty of the workers' committees to promote a good understanding among the workers and between the workers and their employers. It must bring to the employers' notice all suggestions, wishes and complaints of the workers referring to the organisation of the business, the wages and the other matters concerning workers and their welfare, and must give its opinion on them.

Questions

*1. (i)   Explain the meaning of the phrase 'general mobilisation' as used in Source A. (2 marks)
    (ii) What 'other purposes' is Asquith referring to in Source D? (2 marks)
2.   What do Sources A and B reveal about the preparation and implementation of mobilisation orders in Russia? (4 marks)
3.   Does Asquith's threat in Source D demonstrate the failure of recruitment campaigns such as Source C? (4 marks)
4.   How far do Sources D, E and F demonstrate that the war was involving society to an unprecedented level in the war effort?
5.   In light of your own knowledge and the Sources, assess the significance of government action in ensuring effective mobilisation of manpower.

Worked answer

*1. [Questions asking for definitions or explanations of meaning should be answered in as much depth and detail as the number of marks indicates.]

(i) 'General mobilisation' in this context means the full mobilisation of the whole Russian army towards both the German and Austro-Hungarian borders. The Tsar had hoped to send Russian troops only against the Austrians in a 'partial mobilisation' and thus avoid conflict with Germany, but he was persuaded by his generals that the disruption caused by such a move would destroy any possibility of preparing the army to fight Germany.

(ii) The 'other purposes' that Asquith refers to are those reserved occupations such as skilled work in munitions and the engineering trades, which were crucial for the war economy of Great Britain. When workers in these occupations had volunteered for the army in 1914, it had left the British economy in difficulty, and they had to be 'combed out' of the army, to keep up the supply of war materials. These men were exempt from the Military Service Act when it was introduced in 1916.

SOURCES

2. PROPAGANDA

Source G: from a sermon preached by Arthur Winnington-Ingram, Bishop of London, 1915.

And first we see Belgium stabbed in the back and ravaged and then Serbia, and then the Armenian nation wiped out – five hundred thousand at a moderate estimate being actually killed: and then as a necessary consequence, to save the freedom of the world, to save Liberty's own self, to save the honour of women and children, everything that is noblest in Europe, everything that loves freedom and honour, everyone that puts principle above ease, and life itself beyond mere living, are banded in a great crusade – we cannot deny it – to kill Germans: to kill them not for the sake of killing, but to save the world; to kill the good as well as the bad, to kill the young men as well as the old, to kill those who have shown kindness to our wounded as well as those fiends who crucified the Canadian sergeant, who superintended the Armenian massacres, who sank the Lusitania, and who turned the machine guns on the civilians of Aerschott and Louvain – and to kill them lest the civilisation of the world should itself be killed.

Source H: from 'Im Deutschen Wald' by R. H. Heybrodt, 1915.

If Jesus of Nazareth, who preached the love of enemies, were again among us in the flesh – nowhere would he rather be incarnate than in Germany – where do you think he would be found? Do you think he would be standing in a pulpit and saying angrily: 'You sinful Germans, love your enemies'? Certainly not. Instead, he would be right in front, in the first ranks of the sword-bearers who are fighting with implacable hatred. This is where he would be, and he would bless the bleeding hands and the death-dealing weapons, would perhaps himself grasp a sword of judgement and drive the enemies of the Germans farther and farther from the frontiers of the Promised Land, as once he drove the Jewish merchants and usurers out of the Temple.

Source I: from the Bryce Report, 1915.

It is proved –

(i) That there were in many parts of Belgium deliberate and systematically organised massacres of the civil population, accompanied by many isolated murders and other outrages.

(ii) That in the conduct of the war generally, innocent civilians, both men and women, were murdered in large numbers, women violated, and children murdered.

(iii) That looting, house burning, and the wanton destruction of property were ordered and countenanced by the officers of the German Army, that elaborate provisions had been made for systematic incendiarism at the very outbreak of the war, and that the burnings and destruction were frequent where no military necessity could be alleged, being indeed part of a system of general terrorisation.

(iv) That the rules and usages of war were frequently broken, particularly by the using of civilians, including women and children, as a shield for advancing forces exposed to fire, to a less degree by killing the wounded and prisoners, and in the frequent abuse of the Red Cross and the White Flag.

Sensible as they are of the gravity of these conclusions, the Committee conceive that they would be doing less than their duty if they failed to record them as fully established by the evidence. Murder, lust, and pillage prevailed over many parts of Belgium on a scale unparalleled in any war between civilised nations during the last three centuries.

Source J: from the Manifesto of the 93 German intellectuals to the civilized world.

As representatives of German Science and Art, we hereby protest to the civilised world against the lies and calumnies with which our enemies are endeavouring to stain the honour of Germany in her hard struggle for existence – in a struggle that has been forced on her.

It is not true that Germany is guilty of having caused this war. Neither the people, the Government, nor the 'Kaiser' wanted war . . . .

It is not true that we trespassed in neutral Belgium. It has been proved that France and England had resolved on such a trespass, and it has likewise been proved that Belgium had agreed to their doing so. It would have been suicide on our part not to have been beforehand.

It is not true that the life and property of a single Belgian citizen was injured by our soldiers without the bitterest defence having made it necessary . . . .

It is not true that our troops treated Louvain brutally. Furious inhabitants having treacherously fallen upon them in their quarters, our troops with aching hearts were obliged to fire a part of the town, as punishment. The greatest part of Louvain has been preserved . . . .

It is not true that our warfare pays no respects to international laws. It knows no undisciplined cruelty. But in the east, the earth is saturated with the blood of women and children unmercifully butchered by the wild Russian troops, and in the west, dumdum bullets mutilate the breasts of our soldiers . . . .

Have faith in us! Believe, that we shall carry on this war to the end as a civilised nation, to whom the legacy of a Goethe, a Beethoven, and a Kant, is just as sacred as its own hearths and homes.

Source K: from a British leaflet dropped into German trenches by balloon, 1917.

They tell you that you are fighting for the Fatherland. Have you ever thought why you are fighting?

You are fighting to glorify Hindenburg, to enrich Krupp. You are struggling for the Kaiser, the Junkers, and the militarists . . . .

They promise you victory and peace. You poor fools! It was promised your comrades for more than three years. They have indeed found peace, deep in the grave, but victory did not come!

It is for the Fatherland . . . . But what is your Fatherland? Is it the Crown Prince who offered up 600,000 men at Verdun? Is it Hindenburg, who with Ludendorff is many kilometres behind the front lines making more plans to give the English more cannon fodder? Is it Krupp for whom each year of war means millions of marks? Is it the Prussian Junkers who still cry over your dead bodies for more annexations?

No, none of these is the Fatherland. You are the Fatherland. . . . The whole power of the Western world stands behind England and France and America! An army of ten million is being prepared; soon it will come into the battle. Have you thought of that, Michel?

Source L: from *Goodbye to All That* by Robert Graves, 1929.

It never occurred to me that newspapers and statesmen could lie. I forgot my pacifism – I was ready to believe the worst of the Germans. I was outraged to read of the cynical violation of Belgian neutrality. I wrote a poem promising vengeance for Louvain. I discounted perhaps 20 per cent of the atrocity details as wartime exaggeration. That was not, of course, enough.

Source M: from *Mein Kampf* by Adolf Hitler, 1925.

The great majority of a nation is so feminine in its character and outlook that its thought and conduct are ruled by sentiment rather than by sober reasoning. This sentiment, however, is not complex, but simple and consistent. It is not highly differentiated, but has only the negative and positive notions of love and hatred, right and wrong, truth and falsehood. Its notions are never partly this and partly that. English propaganda especially understood this in a marvellous way and put what they understood into practice.

Questions

1. (i) Explain the reference to 'the Armenian massacres' in Source G. (2 marks)
    (ii) Who was 'Krupp' (Source K)? (1 mark)
2. In what ways do Sources G and H employ similar propaganda techniques? (4 marks)
*3. How effectively does Source J refute the allegations made in Source I? (6 marks)
4. How far do Robert Graves's comments in Source L suggest that Hitler's theory of propaganda (Source M) was correct? (4 marks)
5. With reference to all the Sources and drawing on your own knowledge, do you agree that the Allies' propaganda was more successful than the Germans'? (8 marks)

Worked answer

*3. *[If one is asked how effectively one source refutes another, it is crucial that each allegation in the first source is looked at in turn alongside the reply in the second. The issue of effectiveness is ultimately* *subjective, but if certain allegations are not answered or admitted, then it will have to be judged as a poor defence. In such a detailed examination of a source, it is always advisable to support your answer with quotes from the sources.]*

Source J begins with a blanket denial of all the crimes of which Germany is accused. This contrasts poorly with the far more specific allegations in Source I. The accusations in Source I concerning the mistreatment of civilians, especially women and children, are broadly denied in Source J when it is stated that, 'It is not true that the life and property of a single Belgian citizen was injured by our soldiers without the bitterest defence having made it necessary.' This seems to admit that deaths and injuries did take place among Belgian *'franc-tireurs'*, but fails to account for the alleged brutality towards women and children.

The only specific allegation which Source J responds to is the destruction of Louvain, and here again the German intellectuals are forced to partially admit the crime of which their nation is accused, as it is stated that 'our troops with aching hearts were obliged to fire a part of the town'. One is left to consider why other specific allegations are not denied.

Source J prefers to rely on the appeal that these German intellectuals are telling the truth due to their commitment to the high arts and the legacy of German culture. Although the compilers of the Bryce Report failed to visit the site of the alleged massacres, they did interview witnesses and carry out the procedures of a seemingly impartial investigation. The German intellectuals' manifesto is, however, clearly compiled by non-combatants with no access to the relevant evidence. Their denials of German war crimes are predicated on the assumption of total German innocence, which in the context of war is unlikely to be true of any army, and which was certainly not true in the case of the German invasion and occupation of Belgium. The manifesto only manages to escape from the Allies' agenda when it makes counter-claims against the Russian army. As a refutation, it seems ill-advised, appearing elitist, condescending and unconvincing.

3

TOTAL WAR – ECONOMIC MOBILISATION AND THE WAR ECONOMY

BACKGROUND NARRATIVE

When the 'War of Movement' ceased in the winter of 1914, it became clear that victory would depend upon the ability of a country to mobilise its economic and human resources. The appalling slaughter of 1915, and the strains which this new kind of warfare placed upon the participants only served to reinforce this message.

In the spring of 1915, the Western Allies undertook huge offensives at Ypres, Champagne and Artois. These failed to achieve the expected breakthrough, at a cost of more than a million British, French and German casualties. Newspaper headlines in Britain screamed 'Need For Shells: British Attacks Checked: Limited Supply The Cause'.[1] Meanwhile, the first steps towards planning a wartime economy had been taken in Germany, and the results were apparent on the Eastern Front where, between April and June, the German offensive in Galicia drove the hapless Russian army 200 miles back, expelling Russian troops from all the territory occupied in 1914, and capturing Warsaw and much of Russian Poland. This reinforced the (not always accurate) impression that the German war effort was more effectively organised than that of her rivals and forced the Allies to embark upon a more comprehensive mobilisation of their economic resources, which often seemed to follow the Germans' direction.

In Germany, Walther Rathenau, President of the huge electrical combine AEG, had in 1908 predicted a long war of attrition, writing, 'Modern wars will no longer be decided by the hand-to-hand fights of homeric heroes. . . . The War God of our times is economic power.' On 3 August 1914, he persuaded Falkenhayn's War Ministry to set up the War Raw Materials Department (the KRA – *Kriegsrohstoffabteilung*) with Rathenau as director. The KRA prioritised war production; all essential raw materials (including labour) were declared 'emergency materials', on which the military had first claim. Shortage materials would be procured in foreign or occupied countries, and support was provided to German scientists in developing *ersatz* (substitute) products. A series of War Raw Materials Companies were established to administer the production and distribution of particular products, and Rathenau's network of industrial contacts ensured the partici-pation of the whole of German industry, co-opting onto the War Raw Materials Companies the bosses of Germany's biggest firms. These committees, although closely supervised and protected by the state, built upon the existing organisation of German industry, which was dominated by large-scale monopolistic cartels. There was no need, for example, to found a War Coal Company, because there was such a strong coal cartel that one already effectively existed.[2] Alongside this, in September 1914, the biggest German industrial combines formed the War Committee for German Industry, which represented their interests and advised the government on industrial matters.

Germany still needed to import coal and other shortage materials. Faced with an effective British naval blockade of all German maritime traffic, the War Ministry created in 1916 a Central Purchasing Company (ZEG – *Zentraleinkauftsgesellschaft*), which purchased in neutral states, notably Holland and Sweden, what Germany could not produce at home. However, the government failed to guarantee the supply of food. With falling harvests and imports impossible, local authorities and the federal government attempted to fix maximum retail prices for food and clothing. In January 1915, the Imperial Grain Office introduced bread rationing, followed by the rationing of all foodstuffs.

Germany's rapid reorganisation of her economy served as a model for her enemies. The French Minister for War, Millerand, responded to desperate shortages of shells at the Front in September 1914 by reorganising the nation's industry into 12 regions and distributing massive orders for thousands of shells and guns. Although Millerand allowed private business to continue producing armaments, the initiative achieved satisfactory short-term results, significantly increasing French munitions output during the first few months of hostilities. None the less, the munitions shortages of spring 1915 demanded a further increase in production. In May, Albert Thomas was recalled from active service and appointed Under-Secretary of State for Artillery and Munitions (later Minister for Armaments). He established sub-committees co-ordinating specific areas of armaments production, including shells and explosives, and worked closely with French industry which had, in the meantime, organised itself for war.

Meanwhile Britain suffered serious shortages of shells during 1914–15. Despite the passage of DORA in August 1914, the economic demands of war were at first met through a market economy, with the government as customer dispensing lucrative contracts to private industry. Most military experts, however, had anticipated a war of movement and had thus not prioritised the role of heavy artillery. When trench warfare developed, the need for large calibre, high explosive shells became pressing. The army had few such guns and therefore few such shells, and the existing munitions factories, with their ill-trained workers and ill-organised processes, were not capable of such an extremely dangerous, highly skilled enterprise. By spring 1915, Britain was producing only 700 shells per day, whilst Germany produced 250,000![3] The 'shells crisis' surrounding the offensives at Festubert and Neuve Chapelle brought matters to a head, provoking demands for greater central direction of labour and industry.

In May 1915, the Chancellor of the Exchequer, Lloyd George, was appointed Minister of Munitions, with responsibility for delivering adequate military supplies for the Front. He brought energy and determination to his post, setting in place a series of organisations to centrally direct war production. The 'Munitions of War Act', which became law two months later, was 'a considerable extension of the Government's powers of economic control',[4] as it not only provided subsidies to allow private firms to increase production, but also gave the ministry power to establish state-owned munitions factories and shipyards with state-of-the-art equipment and production techniques. However, no equipment of any kind produced by the Ministry of Munitions became available until October 1915, and none in any quantity until the spring of 1916. The impact of the reorganisation of supplies was only felt in 1917, and only became decisive in 1918.

Russia entered the war with misplaced confidence. 'Thanks to the industrial boom and the good harvests in the last few years we are completely prepared for, and can withstand without serious upheavals, a protracted war.'[5] However, attempts to manage the war through existing economic and bureaucratic structures proved disastrous.

Russia possessed 4.5 million rifles in 1914, but by 1915 had conscripted 10 million men. Consequently, some soldiers were issued with cudgels and in some units only one in five soldiers had a bayonet. By the end of 1914, front-line troops were without boots, mobile field kitchens or medical supplies. The shortage of heavy artillery pieces and shells was desperate. Existing government suppliers received huge orders for war materials, but this was insufficient to meet demand. The transition to war production was halting, and mobilisation robbed industry of 40 per cent of its skilled workers, which hit production during the first year of the war. Moreover, railway transport was requisitioned by the army, leaving raw materials sitting idle in sidings.

Russia's 'Great Retreat' of 1915 led to the fall of Warsaw and the loss of Russia's biggest manufacturer of railway locomotives and rolling stock, Levenstein's. Fifty per cent of Russia's railway network fell into German hands, and 4,000 factories were lost (20 per cent of Russia's entire industrial base). Critics demanded that the government take into partnership the Duma, private industry, the Union of Zemstva and Zemgor. Nicholas responded by dismissing Sukhomlinov and granting Zemgor powers to direct light industry and rural workers and to supply the army. A Central War Industries Committee was set up to co-ordinate heavy industry. Special Committees for Defence, Food, Fuel and Transportation directed the production and supply of these essentials.

By the end of 1915, wholesale industrial mobilisation for 'total war' was under way in every state. The fruits of this would be felt in the disastrous campaigns of 1916, when the titans threw their assembled industrial and military might at one another in the mud of Verdun, the Somme and on the Eastern Front.

ANALYSIS 1: HOW EFFECTIVELY DID THE POWERS RESTRUCTURE THEIR ECONOMIES TO MEET THE DEMANDS OF WAR BETWEEN 1914 AND 1918?

Nowhere during the early years of war did the state assume complete authority to dictate the response of industry and society. Old habits died hard, and there was considerable ideological resistance to state intervention in the economy, not least amongst industrialists who wished to retain control of their businesses and profits. Furthermore, 1914 had witnessed widespread 'self-mobilisation' by the civilian population in every state, fuelled by patriotism and propaganda. Consequently, as Hardach has shown, during the first months of war, 'economies continued to function as in peacetime' and 'this discrepancy between military and economic mobilisation sooner or later led to "munitions crises"'.[6] Governments gradually realised that *this* war necessitated a more thoroughgoing reorganisation of economic structures and significant state direction and planning. The same issues arose everywhere – the mobilisation of industry and society; the acquisition of a steady supply of raw materials and the financing of the war. Although 'economic mobilisation' ultimately took similar forms in each country, Germany, and to an extent France, responded with greater urgency to the situation of 1914 than either Britain or Russia.

Germany's wartime reorganisation was directed by the War Ministry, and this caused initial confusion, as the regional Army Corps districts, which formed the administrative units of wartime Germany, did not correspond with the civilian local government regions of pre-war Germany. Consequently, overlapping jurisdictions and the duplication of personnel and function resulted in chaos, exacerbated, at least initially, by the plethora of central agencies created to co-ordinate aspects of the war economy. Given the 'bureaucratic wonderland'[7] that resulted, it is remarkable how successful the KRA proved. Rathenau's creation enabled Germany to raise production levels and direct scarce resources to war industries, and provided the investment necessary to develop the Haber-Bosch process, enabling the large-scale production of ammonia for explosives and fertilisers. Despite the bureaucratic difficulties encountered, the 'corporatist alliance' between the War Ministry and big business prevented Germany from suffering the type of munitions shortage that crippled Russia in 1915. Chickering describes the KRA as 'the most successful economic organisation created . . . during the war'.[8] Its sister agency, the ZEG, however, only partially overcame shortages of material. Iron was obtained from Scandinavia, but shortages bedevilled German producers none the less. The British blockade reduced Hamburg, one of the busiest ports in Europe before the war, to a virtual ghost town and, for all the efforts of Rathenau, German industrial output as a whole fell during the war.

Every other belligerent power experienced desperate 'munitions crises' during 1915. In France, the national daily production of shells in August 1914 was a mere 13,000, but the army demanded 100,000.[9] By January 1915, a combination of state-owned enterprises (generally producing small arms and explosives) and private businesses (producing artillery and shells) spectacularly increased French munitions output.[10] Giant armaments manufacturers like Le Creusot and St Chamond headed up 'production groups', co-ordinated by the *Comité des Forges*, which negotiated contracts with the government on behalf of their members, and embedded itself firmly in the machinery of wartime government. This close relationship ensured industry a powerful voice defending its own interests whilst achieving impressive increases in war production.

Despite Thomas's greater central direction of the war effort, the government remained essentially a customer, and industry 'self-mobilised' during 1914–17. No factories were requisitioned, although the state had established its right to do so in August 1914, and industry's huge profits remained untouched by punitive taxes.

Raw materials remained a problem however. The German occupation of the industrial north deprived France of 74 per cent of her coal and 83 per cent of her iron. Production was relocated to more protected areas, and existing plants increased their output, but, ultimately, France depended upon imported raw materials from Britain for the duration of the war. None the less, as the war progressed, France manufactured the bulk of the munitions deployed by the Allied powers, a notable achievement.

In Britain, Lloyd George's Ministry of Munitions encouraged co-operation between workers and employers. Business leaders such as Sir Eric Geddes, chief manager of the North Eastern Railway, were recruited as senior administrators. Private firms were pushed to amalgamate and carry out research and development on a scale impossible under the normal competitive conditions of a peacetime economy. Trade union leaders were consulted, and accepted the suspension of the right to strike and restrictive trade union rules in the munitions industry for the duration of the war, in return for restrictions on wartime profits. This permitted semi-skilled workers to carry out jobs previously reserved for certain skilled craftsmen, and complex tasks could be broken down into smaller simpler operations ('dilution'), thus opening the way for a rapid recruitment of munitions workers, especially women. However, the ministry was unable to extend its powers into every sector of the economy; for example in shipbuilding, where the dangerous nature of the industry precluded the wholesale employment of women, and the employers and trade unionists resisted dilution. Despite this, the achievement of the ministry remains impressive. From August 1914 to June 1915, the army received 110 artillery pieces, but in the first year of the ministry's existence, 5,006 were produced. Similarly, grenade production increased in the same period from 68,000 to 27 million.

In Russia, following the humiliation in Galicia, the newspaper *The Russian Morning* demanded the mobilisation of all industry 'without delay'.[11] The Association of Industry and Trade joined the attack, pressing the Tsar to 'organise the unutilised power of Russian industry'.[12] Under extreme pressure, Nicholas appointed Gutchkov to co-ordinate the work of War Industries Committees, on which the government, the Central War Industries Committee and Zemgor were all represented. This, and the invitation to Zemgor to provide welfare and medical supplies for the front-line troops, reflected his (belated) acceptance that this war required a more collaborative effort between government and people.

Consequently, by 1916 Russian industrial output was 21 per cent greater than in 1914. However some industries, including militarily significant areas like cotton, actually experienced falling production, resulting partly from difficulties in obtaining raw materials and partly through the loss of so many skilled workers.

Russia's difficulty lay not in production but in transporting materiel to the industrial areas. The loss of western railways and the commandeering of all available rolling stock to supply the Front meant that, by January 1916, the railway system had been stretched to breaking point. In all, 575 stations had closed due to maintenance problems and the Moscow–Archangel line was so over-burdened that it could not cope with demand; 150,000 wagons stood loaded but idle, although Norman Stone argues that this arose more from timetabling problems, organisational failure and shortages of skilled labour than from want of locomotives.[13] Fish, grain and vegetables rotted in sidings whilst the big cities, swollen by refugees, ran desperately short of food. Petrograd received 25 per cent of the grain it needed in February 1917. As Kennedy observes, 'These infrastructural inadequacies could not be overcome by Russia's minuscule and ineffective bureaucracy.'[14]

Historians broadly agree that Russia's munitions crisis resulted almost wholly from mismanagement by the Tsar and his ministers and the government's failure to recruit assistance from private industry, although industry was undeniably backward, compared to Germany. In Britain and France, it was an inability to abandon the ideology of the *laissez-faire* liberal economy which hindered effective industrial mobilisation. Only the failure of the Artois offensive and Britain's notorious shell shortage persuaded the Allies to act. The simultaneous appointments in May 1915 of Lloyd George in Britain and Albert Thomas in France reflect the decision to mobilise the nation in a more systematic and centralised fashion. Hereafter, Germany's initial advantages evaporated in the face of the Allies' superior economic resources and Britain's effective naval blockade.

The war placed unprecedented demands upon the finances of the belligerent nations, whilst simultaneously impeding the flow of international trade. Nowhere were these problems greater than in Russia. With the outbreak of war, all trade with Germany (39 per cent of Russia's total foreign trade)[15] ceased and the Central Powers' blockade of Russian maritime movement in the Baltic and Black Seas slashed Russian exports by almost 90 per cent. However, Russia continued to import essential munitions and machine tools, resulting in a net trade deficit for the war years of 2.5 billion roubles. Furthermore, the state lost valuable tariff revenues. Russian politicians fully appreciated the implications of this: 'The economic isolation of our country is one of the most painful and dangerous aspects of the war.'[16] The crisis was accentuated by the Tsar's extraordinary decision in August 1914 to ban the sale of vodka, the national drink, on which the state had possessed a monopoly, thereby depriving himself of 678 million roubles per annum. Duma politicians were flabbergasted, as they had just raised the vodka duty in order to increase the state's wartime revenues! One critic noted 'Never, since the dawn of human history, has a single country, in time of war, renounced the principal source of its revenue '.[17] By 1915, state finances were in ruins. Since the taxing of excessive war profits was resisted by powerful industrial interests, the government met its financial obligations by borrowing, issuing War Bonds, abandoning the Gold Standard and printing more money, which resulted in hyperinflation. Consequently, the National Debt, relatively manageable in 1914 (8.8 billion roubles) swelled to 43 billion by 1916.

Things were remarkably similar in Germany, where war finance was perhaps the biggest failure of the government. By 1915, with the war costing 3 billion Reichsmarks a month, only 16 per cent of the cost was met by taxation. Instead, from the outset, Minister of Finance Helferrich authorised the Reichsbank to print more banknotes and to repeatedly issue Treasury notes to investors through the Imperial Loan Fund. Thus the regime covered the revenue shortfall by printing more money and increasing borrowing. Sales of War Bonds raised around 100 billion marks by 1918, but these policies resulted in accelerating inflation and an enormous national debt, which by 1918 had reached 150 billion

Reichsmarks. However, German industry obstructed any taxation of their enormous profits. Although some local and regional authorities did increase local taxes, it was 1916 before the federal government introduced any new taxation to pay for the war: a minimal tax on 'excess profits', which raised only 7.3 billion Reichsmarks. The financial measures taken during the war are neatly summarised by Helferrich: 'We can cling to the hope that, once peace has been concluded, we can present our enemies with the bill for this war which has been forced upon us.'[18]

France witnessed similar problems. Although the government anticipated in July 1914 the likely financial demands of the forthcoming war, and approved the introduction of income tax, they bizarrely delayed its introduction until 1919, reasoning that it would damage morale. Consequently, France, like Germany, fell back on borrowing. 'National Defence Bonds' were issued, at 5 per cent interest, raising vital revenue but contributing to a growing debt problem. France became increasingly dependent on British and American credit, without which she might have been bankrupted long before 1918. From July 1917, France received an American subsidy of $160 million per month. By the end of the war, even the National Defence Bonds were undersubscribed. Indeed, Bernard and Dubief note that, whilst 'the French continued to give their own and their children's blood freely, they were the most reluctant of all nations to give their money'.[19]

From August 1914 to April 1917, Britain acted as principal banker and loan-raiser for the Allies, raising loans for France, Italy and Russia as well as financing her own war effort. In order to pay for this, War Savings Certificates and Bonds were sold, and taxation was dramatically increased. During the first year of the war, three war budgets raised income tax by nearly 150 per cent, and by the end of the war it stood at 6 shillings in the pound, an 800 per cent increase on the rate in August 1914. Tax thresholds were lowered, and as wages rose, more people paid. The supposedly ineffective excess profits duty raised £200–300 million a year. Indirect taxes were raised or introduced on a range of consumer goods. Despite all this, the government was forced to sell 25 per cent of overseas investments to meet the spiralling costs of the war (£7 million a day by 1917) and still fell short. Borrowing, particularly from the United States, was the only answer.

Germany was better placed than her rivals to adapt to the changing conditions of the first year of war, due to the cartelisation of her industry and her authoritarian political culture. Many of the ideological obstacles which held Britain back in the early months of the war were looser in Germany; and in Rathenau, Germany possessed an able administrator, with excellent connections in both industry and government. Her enemies were less generously blessed, although, as we have seen, France's efforts to increase armaments production between August 1914 and May 1915 were moderately successful. After the munitions crises of spring 1915, output in every state rose, and the crises of 1915 were not repeated the following year, when even in the Russian army 'all the units at the Front possess their full complement of rifles'.[20] Once industrial mobilisation was under way in all three Allied states, Germany's initial technical and military superiority was gradually eroded, and this forced the army to begin to contemplate more radical measures, such as the Hindenburg Programme of 1916. The reality was, however, that a protracted war favoured the Western Allies, whose combined economic potential and access to overseas supplies from their colonies, the British Commonwealth and North America, would enable them to outproduce Germany in the long run.

Questions

1. In what ways did the First World War place new strains upon the state and the economy?
2. Why was Germany more successful than her enemies in mobilising her economy and society during the first year of the war?

ANALYSIS (2): WHAT IMPACT DID THE WAR HAVE ON LIVING STANDARDS IN EUROPE?

Probably the most damaging consequence of the war for the civilian populations of Europe was its impact upon food supplies and the cost of living. Whilst both sides reorganised to meet the war's industrial demands, only the Western Allies effectively supplied their people with food and the other essentials of life. The desperate consequences of the German and Russian governments' failure to guarantee the food supply may be seen as central to their ultimate defeat. Indeed Jay Winter asserts that Britain and France's ability to sustain and even improve material conditions of life during wartime, set against the manifest failure of the Central Powers to do so, was 'one of the pre-requisites of victory'.[21]

Even before 1914, Germany had imported 30 per cent of all foodstuffs. The war brought about a further 30 per cent fall in production, due principally to labour shortages and the effects of the British naval blockade. Although the government concluded that the wartime food supply would still be sufficient, given the excessive consumption of the average pre-war German,[22] this overlooked the privileged access to

Germany's limited food supplies enjoyed by the military and the rural population. Consequently, urban-dwellers experienced almost immediate shortages, and prices rose by almost 100 per cent in the first year of the war. Official responses were confused and contradictory. Attempts by local authorities to fix maximum retail prices for food and clothing were duplicated by central government agencies like the Imperial Grain Office which, in January 1915, introduced bread rationing. The *Schweinenmord* ('pig-killing') of April 1915, however, simply caused a temporary glut of pork and deprived German farmers of valuable animal fertiliser. Moreover, only half-hearted attempts were made to encourage Germans to renounce meat and fats and consume more vegetables and grains. The creation of the War Food Office, in June 1916, didn't improve matters. Its imposition of steadily lower rations of all foodstuffs, and its manipulation of prices, only encouraged farmers to feed their produce to their animals or to deal with black-marketeers.

The 1915 harvest was 2.5 million tonnes below expectations. Shortly afterwards meat began to disappear from shops and women in Berlin camped out in front of markets and warehouses to obtain vegetables. In Leipzig, by June 1916 there was 'no butter or fat of any sort, and practically no meat and potatoes have quite given out'.[23] Cloth, leather and oil grew short and observers noted that shops contained last year's goods, which remained unsold due to a simultaneous collapse of supply and demand. Coal shortages in January 1916 resulted in reduced domestic supplies. Warm clothing was hard to come by, and hostels were opened to warm the elderly. A shortage of soap, and the closure of public baths for want of fuel, made it harder to maintain personal cleanliness.

Such shortages undermined public health and eroded morale. A black market operated among rich civilians and senior army officers. Elegant hotels like the Esplanade continued to serve beef, fruit and coffee. Meanwhile, faced with inadequate official rations (which fell to 1,100 calories in July 1917), German citizens supplemented their diet illegally. Formerly law-abiding citizens ran smuggling rings and shop-lifted, and millions of Germans with relatives in the country paid them regular visits ('*hamsterfahren*') in order to beg a little extra food, which they stockpiled. Perhaps one-third of food consumed was obtained in this way, but the need to resort to such expedients, illegal in wartime Germany, was deeply resented.

In 1916, heavy rains and blight ruined the potato harvest – a disaster because so many German workers depended upon it for their diet. The result was the 'turnip winter'. The ubiquitous turnip appeared in every foodstuff, from soup to bread to coffee. Three thousand public kitchens were set up to serve workers and their children, but workers' daily calorific intake slumped alarmingly. A Dusseldorf worker in January 1917 consumed only 30 per cent of the calorific intake of a workhouse inmate of 1900. Germans survived the 'turnip winter' on less than 1,300 calories per day, and eggs, cheese and beer disappeared altogether from their diet.[24] One doctor observed, 'Slowly but surely we are slipping into a now still well-organised famine.'[25] The civilian mortality rate climbed rapidly. In 1916, 121,000 civilians died, and in 1918, a year of epidemics and desperate shortages, 293,000 died.

Yet the German people did not starve. The War Committee for Consumer Interests (KAKI) concluded that 'calorie intake had fallen by more than a fifth . . . but was still quite close to recommended standards'.[26] However, episodic hunger undermined morale. The Deputy Commanding Generals reported, in July 1918, that 'economic conditions, and primarily the food situation, were decisive for the general state of mind'.[27]

Although workers in essential war industries were to some extent cushioned from the inflationary effects of shortages, since their wages rose more rapidly than others', fixed-income middle-class groups and 'civilian' workers saw the value of their incomes eroded. Real wages inexorably declined, on average by 30 per cent.[28] Resentment of the war leadership and of profiteers spread. Most of all, bitterness focused on the government's failure to ensure equality of sacrifice.

Things were, if anything, worse in Russia. Six million refugees from occupied Russia swelled the population of Petrograd and Moscow. Accommodation became hard to find, and there was intense competition for unskilled work, food and fuel. Furthermore, due to the collapse of the transportation system, the substantial rural food surpluses could not reach the cities. Prices for basic necessities like coal and bread spiralled upwards, yet bread rationing was only introduced in March 1917. This was too little too late. Daily bread consumption per head in January 1916 was 2.7 lb. By March 1917 it had fallen to 1.8 lb. Meanwhile the Tsar exhorted workers, as their patriotic duty, to labour longer hours than ever before for no extra wages. Average monthly wages for industrial workers did rise, but, crucially, workers in munitions and metal factories earned perhaps 50 per cent more than those in 'civilian' industries or on fixed salaries. Prices climbed much faster, milk by 150 per cent, bread by 500 per cent and clothing by 500 per cent. Moscow rents were 400 per cent higher than before the war. Once inflation had done its work, real wages declined for all workers.[29]

Fuel shortages brought suffering during the cold winter of 1916–17. In Odessa, the electric power station closed, resulting in the suspension of the water supply, street-car services and municipal bathhouses.[30] This was all the more insufferable because the rich were so obviously not sharing the pain. Permits for wine and liquor could be bought from corrupt officials, and in smarter restaurants the alcohol ban was quietly ignored. The black market thrived. The ballet was still popular, the rich bought diamonds to insure themselves against the collapsing currency, and the court jeweller Fabergé continued to do good business.

The impact of the war upon rural Russia is more difficult to assess. Perhaps 50 per cent of the male rural workforce was conscripted, and over 5 million horses were requisitioned, yet the area under peasant cultivation actually rose, although the area under cultivation by larger landowners fell, due to a shortage of wage labourers. The German block- ade prevented the importation of fertilisers, machinery and even basic tools. None the less, falling production was balanced by the fact that Russia could no longer export grain, so there was actually a surplus in the 1914 and 1915 harvests. However, the prioritisation of military needs meant that few goods were produced for civilian consumption. This discouraged the peasants from selling their grain, as they could not spend their earnings. Instead they hoarded produce, ate it themselves, and fed their animals with it, whilst the cities went hungry.

France witnessed similar strains but coped rather better with the pressures on food supply and living standards. Perhaps 5 million peasants were conscripted during the war and, despite heroic efforts by those they left behind, grain production fell during the war years by 30 per cent to 58 million tonnes in 1916.[31] In one village 'by the second year of the war there were already some properties without farmers and at the beginning of the third year there were four abandoned properties'.[32] However, falling output was offset by rising prices, so that one con- temporary complained 'the farmers have grown rich'.[33] Yet, although discontent regarding the availability and price of food was voiced, the situation never became desperate. The state offset food shortages by obtaining imports, and market gardening was encouraged. Observers noted voluntary restrictions on consumption. Shortages of fuel were more serious, and rents rose to unacceptable levels, provoking discontent and protests.

Shortages led to inflation, which, by 1918, had reduced average real wages by about 20 per cent. This, however, conceals wide fluctuations between regions and industries. Paris suffered particularly severely and, as elsewhere, munitions workers earned better wages than 'civilian' industries. Suddenly rising prices between March and May 1917 contributed to the catastrophic collapse of public morale that provoked the strike movement of 1917. The price of fresh vegetables rose by

100 per cent between 1914 and March 1917, but the next eight weeks saw a further 300 per cent increase. In the same period, meat prices rose by 47 per cent, and coal doubled in price. By the end of 1917, the people, especially in Paris, were struggling against desperate economic conditions. The 'Confidential Bulletin' reported that 'Among white-collar workers, petty officials and the lower middle classes one . . . finds symptoms of anxiety', and observed that 'domestic calm and tranquillity cannot be maintained if there are bread shortages'.[34]

However, the food supply was restored, with British assistance, and rebellion averted. Ultimately there was no recourse to bread rationing in France, and conditions, whilst difficult, never became desperate. There is little doubt that the resilience of the French people, and the maintenance of decent standards of living during the conflict, owed much to the state's determined preservation of wage levels, workers' rights and food supplies.[35] Encouraged by the government, some employers provided canteens, crèches, housing for workers and infirmaries. Others supported workers' own co-operatives. Family allowances were put in place in several industries, including mining and the railways. The 'allocation militaire', amounting to 1.50 fr and 50 centimes per child, paid by the state to the dependants of front-line soldiers, mitigated some of the worst effects of their lost wages. One *préfet* observed that 'in providing everyone with the necessities of life it has been the main cause of domestic peace and calm'.[36] The flood of women into the factories also enabled many families to preserve their pre-war incomes and living standards. Consequently, France witnessed only a marginal increase in the civilian death rate (4.5 per cent), whereas in Germany the death rate rose by a third.

Britain witnessed perhaps the least disruption to civilian society during the war. Living standards were maintained and the centralised distribution of food supplies and rationing ensured that diet and nutrition, notably amongst the poorest in society, improved dramatically.

British workers gained by the war, using their role in war production to force improved pay and conditions, as well as greater participation in government. Employers were encouraged to pay war bonuses by the Ministry of Munitions, which wanted industrial peace so as to maximise production. Collective pay bargaining was actively encouraged by the ministry, and National Pay Awards were introduced for the first time. After 1915, arbitration tribunals were set up to resolve disputes, thereby ensuring negotiated wage rises and uninterrupted production. Even so, workers became aggrieved over the rising cost of living, the increasing 'dilution' of skilled work, through the introduction of unskilled (often female) labour and new, mechanised processes, and the high cost of housing and rents. The wave of strikes on the Clyde during 1915 led Lloyd George to promote the Rent Restrictions Bill at the end of the year, pegging rents at 1914 levels. In 1915, after a period of unchecked price inflation, the state introduced fixed prices for essential foods, so as to maintain morale, and in February 1918, the Minister of Food Lord Rhondda introduced rationing.

For all the government's sincere efforts to mitigate the worst effects of the war, living conditions suffered. Real wages declined.[37] However, for many households, the absence of father or sons at the Front meant that the family income actually went further and resulted in better diet and nutrition. Even so, government initiatives designed to make food stretch further (such as 'meatless days') were often regarded as derisory by the workers (who regularly went meatless). There was resentment at the apparent prosperity of the wealthy amidst the privations of war, and this concern was shared by members of the government. 'Profiteering is rife in every commodity – bread, meat, tea, butter – and the masses are being exploited right and left', observed Lord Devonport.[38]

It is clear that Britain and France looked after their people better. Recent studies suggest that, whilst German children seem to have suffered from declining nutrition and health during the war, British children's diet seems to have improved.[39] But why was this? The principal difference between the Western democracies and the other belligerents appears to have been the establishment of an *effective* system of centrally directed rent controls, subsidies, separation allowances and efficient rationing and food distribution, enabling the preservation of the health and welfare of the population. This was in turn only really possible because the state was prepared, at least partially, to subordinate the interests of business to the needs of the state. Britain's tax on excess profits, for example, prevented industrialists from profiteering on the grand scale that some German firms did.

As the war progressed, Britain and France evolved systems which sustained their large armies and the populations from which they were recruited and equipped, while Germany and Russia failed to do so, resulting in the collapse of civilian and front-line morale. Ultimately, this may explain why the Western Allies were able, during 1918, to rally their exhausted people for one last effort, whereas efforts by the Central Powers and Russia to do so met with sullen compliance, but with little active enthusiasm and support. As Avner Offer asserts, in this respect, it was the provision of 'primary commodities' which decided the outcome of the war.[40]

Questions

1. Consider the view that the working classes made significant gains in every state as a result of the First World War.
2. Why did the war affect the living standards of the British people less severely than the populations of the continental powers?

SOURCES

1. ECONOMIC MOBILISATION

Source A: Rathenau's assessment of the work of the KRA.

If we look at our organisation in its totality and enquire how Germany could succeed where England faltered and Lloyd George failed, I may offer the following answer;

First of all we made an early start. As soon as it was approached, the War Office boldly decided to identify itself with us ... and, in fostering us, the War Office has never failed to exert its power and genius ....

Secondly, our organisation has always remained well-centralised and unified. It has never been turned over to commissions, committees or experts. It has never been de-centralised by bureaucratic methods. There was a central will endowed with authority ....

The third factor is German idealism. A group of men was found ready to trust a common leader, working without remuneration, without contract, impelled by enthusiasm, offering their strength and their intellect because they knew that their country needed them. Co-operating in a spirit of democratic and friendly companionship, frequently working quite independently, this group has created a new economic life for Germany. It had the support of our industry, young and elastic, ready to act, equal to the demands of the time, able to perform what had seemed impossible.

The highest and last factor ... is human trust and confidence. I have to thank three Prussian Ministers of War for the confidence which they have bestowed upon ... our work. It speaks well for the German and the Prussian system that such human relationship could be given and received in the service of our economic life and in defence of our country.

Source B: Rodzianko's observations regarding the organisation of the war effort, arising out of a visit to the HQ of Grand Duke Nicholas, at the Front.

The Grand Duke stated that he was obliged to stop fighting, temporarily, for the lack of ammunition and boots.

'You have influence', he said. 'You are trusted. Try to get boots for the Army, as soon as possible.'

I replied that this could be done if the zemstvos and public organisations were asked to help. There was plenty of material and labour in Russia .... The best thing to do would be to call a congress of the heads of the zemstvos and ask their co-operation. The Grand Duke was greatly pleased with this idea ....

Realising that there might be objections from the government I decided to talk it over with some of the ministers. Krivoshein, Sukhomlinov and Goremykin liked the idea .... My interview with [Interior Minister] Maklakov was quite out of the ordinary. When I explained ... Maklakov said: 'Yes, yes; what you tell me agrees perfectly with the information I get from my agents .... The congress to take up the needs of the army has for its real object to discuss political questions and demand a constitution.'

Source C: statistics: British munitions production, 1914–18.

	1914	1915	1916	1917	1918
Guns	91	3,390	4,314	5,137	8,039
Tanks	–	150	1,110	1,359	
Aircraft	200	1,900	6,100	14,700	32,000
Machine guns	300	6,100	33,500	79,700	120,990

Source D: a modern historian (Chickering) comments on German industrial mobilisation.

The effectiveness of this hastily improvised effort stood out in the annals of Germany's economic mobilisation for war. Despite the anxieties of the War Ministry, the German armies did not collapse in late 1914 for want of weapons or munitions; and in this respect at least, German soldiers were well supplied for the duration of the conflict. There was no munitions crisis in Germany.

Source E: a modern historian (Winter) comments on German industrial mobilisation.

The German war economy presents one of the earliest and least successful examples of a 'military-industrial complex' in action. The corporatist solution to Germany's economic difficulties was no solution at all.

Questions

1. Explain the meaning of the following terms, in the context of these documents:
   (i) 'KRA' (Source A) (2 marks)
   (ii) 'zemstvos' (Source B) (2 marks)
2. Comment on Source A's value to a historian assessing the effectiveness of the KRA during the early years of the war. (4 marks)
3. Do the figures in Source C demonstrate that British industrial mobilisation was ultimately successful? (5 marks)
*4. Compare and contrast the views of the historians Chickering and Winter, in Sources D and E, regarding the success of the KRA. (5 marks)
5. How far do the Sources, and your own knowledge, support the view that all the participants struggled at first to cope with the economic and material demands of the First World War? (7 marks)

Worked answer

*4. In Source D, Chickering gives a largely positive view of the effectiveness of the KRA in reorganising German industry to meet the demands of war, and this contrasts strongly with the view expressed by Winter in Source E. This is partially explicable by the differing focus of the two writers.

Chickering explicitly addresses the early achievements of the KRA, referring to 'late 1914', and the lack of a 'munitions crisis', which implicitly refers to the crises which affected other European states during 1915. He also restricts his positive analysis to the question of munitions and does not deal here with other aspects of the war effort.

Winter, by contrast, looks at the war as a whole, referring generally to the 'German war economy'. He particularly criticises Germany's over-arching approach to economic management (the 'corporatist solution'), which, ultimately, did not provide Germany with the means to sustain the war. It is also worth noting the title of the work from which this extract was taken: a work on the social impact of the war. It could be that Winter's assessment deliberately lays aside Germany's initial success in supplying her armies' munitions needs, because he is more interested in the broader issues.

None the less, it is hard to entirely accept the assessment of the German war effort given by Winter, since, as Chickering observes, her armies never ran short of munitions during the war, despite the scale of the conflict and the size of the alliance ranged against her.

SOURCES

2. THE FOOD SITUATION

Source F: weekly diets for one working-class adult in Germany.

	Hamburg poorhouse 1900	Dusseldorf rations January 1917	Dusseldorf rations April 1918
Potatoes	8.3 lb.	3 lb.	7 lb.
Rye bread	9.6 lb.	3.5 lb. ('war bread')	4 lb. ('war bread')
Meat/sausage	660 g	200 g	200 g
Milk	2,400 g	100 g	216 g (inc. canned milk)
Flour	185 g	120 g ('milling product')	220 g ('milling product')
Butter	260 g	62.5 g (inc. 'fats')	62.5 g (inc. 'fats')
Cheese	60 g	60 g cheese 'spread'	212.5 g mostly 'spread'
Beer	350 g		
Total calorific value of diet	26,500 calories	7,900 calories	11,200 calories
Total protein	1,000 g	260 g	350 g

Source G: 'The Ten Food Commandments' – a German public information leaflet, 1915.

Germany is standing against a World of Enemies who would Destroy Her.

1. They wish to starve us out like a besieged fortress. They will fail because we have enough breadstuffs in the country to feed our population until the next harvest, but nothing must be wasted.
2. Breadstuffs must not be used as fodder.
3. Therefore be economical with bread in order that the hopes of our foes may be confounded.
4. Respect the daily bread, then you will have it always, however long the war may last.
5. Teach these maxims also to your children.

6. Do not despise even a single piece of bread because it is no longer fresh.
7. Do not cut off a slice more than you need to eat. Think always of our soldiers in the field who, often in some far-off, exposed position, would rejoice to have the bread which you waste.
8. Eat War Bread. It is recognisable by the letter K. It satisfies and nourishes as thoroughly as any other kind . . . .
9. Whoever first peels the potatoes before cooking them, wastes much. Therefore cook potatoes with the jackets on . . . .
10. Do not throw away leavings of potatoes, meat, vegetables and so on, which you cannot use, but collect them as fodder for cattle.

Source H: from the diary of an Englishwoman, Princess Blücher, living in Germany during the war.

We are all growing thinner every day and the rounded contours of the German nation have become a legend of the past. We are all gaunt and bony now ... and our thoughts are chiefly taken up with wondering what our next meal will be, and dreaming of the good things that had once existed.

Now one sees faces like masks, blue with cold and drawn with hunger, with the harassed expression common to all those who are continually speculating as to the possibility of another meal.

Source I: a Bolshevik report on the food situation in 1916.

In Bryansk county, Orel province, there is no rye flour, salt, paraffin or sugar ... a pound of sugar costs from one to one ruble fifty. Discontent is rife and more than once there have been strikes on factories and plants with the demand for 'flour and sugar' . . . . I stayed at the town of Zhizdra, Kaluga province. There was an acute shortage of domestic items; at all times there was no flour, sugar and paraffin at all. No commodities other than hay were brought in from the villages. I then travelled around the villages: grumbling, discontent and a vague apprehension all around.

Source J: cost of a Moscow textile worker's daily food basket.

Year	Daily cost (kopeks)	Change (1913 = 100)
1913	24.23	100
1914	26.53	109
1915	31.70	131
1916	49.47	204
1917 (Jan.)	87.51	361

Source K: extract from 'Food for France and Its Public Control'.

The increase in the price for wheat has been balancing almost exactly the decrease in production:

Average price of native wheat	
Before the war	22F per cwt
1914	30F per cwt
1915	36F per cwt
1916	50F per cwt

which means in 1916 an increase of over 50 per cent.

The price of meat has been rising in a similar proportion and an increase of circa 50 per cent may safely be stated as an index for the increase in the prices of all the main foodstuffs.

Questions

1.   (i) What was 'War Bread' (Sources F and G)? (2 marks)
     (ii) What is meant by 'domestic items' (Source I)? (2 marks)
*2. Comment on the reliability of Source H for our understanding of the situation in Germany during the war. (4 marks)
3.   To what extent do Sources I and J support one another regarding the food situation in Russia by 1917? (4 marks)
4.   Does Source K prove that living standards in France were declining? (5 marks)
5.   Using both the Sources and your own knowledge, account for the difficulties experienced by the continental states in maintaining the food supply to the civilian population. (8 marks)

Worked answer

*2. Source H comes from the diary of an Englishwoman resident who, judging from her title, was married to a German aristocrat in Germany during the war. This alone might suggest impartiality, since she clearly has a foot in both camps. Furthermore, her comments reveal that she was aware of the desperate state of the German people ('Now one sees faces like masks, blue with cold and drawn with hunger'), and suggest a sympathy for them, which enhances her value as an impartial witness.

However, we should be cautious regarding the reliability of this writer. Princess Blücher's experience of the war will necessarily have been class-defined. As an aristocrat, she may have been insulated from some of the suffering. It is hard to believe, for example, that she will have had much direct contact with the working-class German, or that she would have been forced to queue for bread with other women. Consequently, we may catch a glimpse of the situation in her diaries, but her distance from the genuinely desperate daily lives of working Germans during the war will make this record only a partial, if sympathetic, one.

4

THE WOMEN'S WAR

BACKGROUND NARRATIVE

For women, the war was a mixed blessing. Whether employed in industrial or agricultural sectors or engaged in domestic service, women still bore principal responsibility in the traditional female sphere and on the home front. They endured the burdens of domestic life, such as queuing for scarce food, especially eggs, meat and sugar, in what German women ironically called 'polonaises'. Although the conflict offered avenues into the workforce, no woman in the Great Powers yet had the right to vote and their wages remained inferior to those of men. In fact, in the early months of the war, due to the economic dislocation, female unemployment in the textiles industry actually rose.

As the war continued and the impact of manpower shortages was felt, both employers and governments became aware of the need to more effectively utilise the female workforce, especially in skilled positions. After 1915, women began to have access to occupations in which they would not previously have been employed. Some took over their husbands' jobs, and became blacksmiths, paper-hangers and grave-diggers. Others took up non-manual trades where women had been rarely employed before the war, such as ambulance drivers and managers. Banks and offices employed women tellers and clerks to do jobs usually reserved for men. In France, government policy resulted in women making up 25 per cent of the personnel in war factories –

a total of 1.6 million female employees. Women in France worked at all levels of every trade, running machines, loading ships, handling shells, control and inspection jobs and delicate machine-calibration. The German government recruited workers in 1917 by offering higher pay and factory housing. In a period of limited separation allowances and a housing shortage, such an approach paid dividends. The number of women employed in German engineering, chemical and metal works was six times greater than that before the war.

In all the Great Powers, nursing had been seen as a suitable role for 'respectable' young women. In this way, many middle- and upper-class women did find unprecedented freedom from the patriarchal home, as well as hard and emotionally demanding work. For example, in Russia, the war emergency opened up a range of new opportunities for women, the most immediately obvious being in the nursing and medical professions. Within weeks of the declaration of war, women were enrolling as Red Cross medical assistants and 'sisters of mercy' and were soon despatched to the Front. Of those who stayed at home, many volunteered for work in infirmaries for wounded soldiers which were set up privately: the Women's Medical Institute in Petrograd set up one themselves, as did the feminist League of Equal Rights.

In Britain, the number of women employed increased from 3,224,600 in July 1914 to 4,814,600 in January 1918. Nearly 200,000 women were employed in government departments, with half a million becoming clerical workers in private offices and a quarter of a million working on the land. The greatest increase of women workers was in engineering. Over 700,000 of these women worked in the highly dangerous munitions industry. Whereas in 1914 there were 212,000 women working in the munitions industry, by the end of the war it had increased to 950,000. Christopher Addison, who succeeded David Lloyd George as Minister of Munitions, estimated in June 1917 that about 80 per cent of all weapons and shells were being produced by 'munitionettes'. The work was extremely dangerous and accidents at munitions factories resulted in over 200 deaths in Britain alone. Others suffered health problems such as TNT poisoning because of the dangerous chemicals the women were using.

The British government decided that more women would have to become more involved in producing food and goods to support their war effort. This included the establishment of the Women's Land Army

(WLA) in 1917, which, despite popular myth, was a relatively unpopular form of war work, only employing 16,000 women in the 1918 harvest. Farmers failed to accept women as acceptable alternative workers to men and most working-class women realised that money could be made (and spent) more easily in towns and cities. A disproportionate number of middle-class women joined the WLA, and found the work exhausting and dangerous, with low pay and poor accommodation.

With heavy losses on the Western Front in 1916, the British army became concerned by its reduced number of fighting soldiers. In January 1917, the government announced the establishment of a new voluntary service, the Women's Auxiliary Army Corps (WAAC). The plan was for these women to serve as clerks, telephonists, waitresses, cooks, and as instructors in the use of gas masks, to replace men who could then be sent to fight at the Front. Women in the WAAC were not given full military status. The women enrolled rather than enlisted and were punished for breaches of discipline by civil rather than military courts. Women in the WAAC were not allowed to hold commissions and so were divided into officials (officers), forewomen (sergeants), assistant forewomen (corporals) and workers (privates). Between January 1917 and the Armistice, over 57,000 women served in the WAAC.

Although not on combat duties, members of the WAAC had to endure shelling from heavy artillery and, during one attack in April 1918, nine WAACs were killed at the Etaples Army Camp. British newspapers claimed that it was another example of a German atrocity but Helen Gwynne-Vaughan, the WAAC's Chief Controller (Overseas), was quick to point out at a press conference that, as the WAAC were in France as replacements for soldiers, the enemy was quite entitled to try and kill them.[1]

In Russia, the active service of women was taken further after the 1917 February Revolution, when the Women's Death Battalion was organised by Maria Bochkareva, who had enlisted in the army in 1914 after petitioning the Tsar, and had been decorated and risen to the rank of sergeant. General Brusilov allowed her to do this in the hope that the example of the women would persuade the rest of the army to keep fighting. The battalion was paraded in Moscow's Red Square in June, dressed in military uniform and shaven-headed, and departed for the front line. During Russia's last offensive that summer, the battalion broke through two lines of German trenches, before being decimated by German fire. The remnants of the force were withdrawn and some were given the duty of guarding the Winter Palace when the Bolsheviks launched their coup in October.[2]

All these changes provoked much comment at the time. Employing women in jobs traditionally done by men presented a challenge to traditional sex roles. Voices were raised about the moral dangers of industrial work, the prospect of child neglect and the physical risks to women's health in factories. It was largely accepted by both men and women that the changes in women's roles were only temporary and that normality would be restored once the war came to an end. However, it was undeniable that in all of Europe women had demonstrated abilities that they had had little opportunity to demonstrate before the war, and this was reflected in the change in attitude towards women's political rights in all the four Great Powers.

ANALYSIS (1): DID THE WAR TRANSFORM THE POSITION OF WOMEN IN SOCIETY?

It is, of course, very difficult to draw conclusions as to the impact of the war on women as a whole, mainly because women's pre-war experience was so widely differentiated according to their class, age group, trade and geographical area. Large numbers of working-class women had worked in factories before and/or during their married lives and an equally large number worked from home in the 'sweated' industries, most notably clothes making. To these women, hard physical labour was not especially novel and any change in their social status was due to a reappraisal of the value of women's work and to their personal experience of work in a larger unit than most women had generally experienced before the war. For middle- and upper-class women, despite the valiant attempts of educationalists and pioneers, 'respectability' meant leaving any job held on marriage (in professions such as teaching, this was compulsory in some countries) and then devoting oneself to bearing and raising children and keeping home for their husbands, unless widowhood, illness or separation forced them back into the workforce. This group, more articulate and more vocal than the workers, experienced the most dramatic shift in personal experience during the war, and their accounts of this experience may have led some early historians to believe talk of a 'revolution' in women's position during the war.[3] Similarly, the press, denied much detail of the fighting, by censorship, seized on stories of women taking on unfamiliar roles and pumped them for their patriotic message to urge others to follow this example.

In France, far from liberating women into a new world of work opportunity, the war marked the end of a trend of high female participation rates in extra-domestic employment, even though historians admit that the reversal of this trend may well have occurred without the experience of war.[4]

The war seems to have had little permanent impact on the numbers of women at work in France. Women already made up 35 per cent of the labour force in 1914 and, while this figure did expand considerably to a peak of 46 per cent in 1918, once the war finished, the figures for female workers reverted to pre-war levels and then continued to decline over the next forty years. In this period, with propaganda urging women to 'work for repopulation',[5] a return to domesticity was the common experience of most French women. The only permanent changes were in certain important professions, such as accountancy, law and medicine, and, even here, the numbers of new female entrants were very small.

In Russia there was no mass mobilisation of women into traditional male industries. Despite the demands of women's organisations, public service and the law remained closed to them. But as the terrible costs of the Eastern Front sucked in more conscripts, employers turned to female labour, which had the added bonus of being cheaper than male. In Petrograd the proportion of women in industry rose from 25 per cent of the total in 1913 to 33 per cent by 1917. In Moscow, where women had been a major part of the workforce for decades, the increase went from 39 to 49 per cent in the same period. In the predominantly agrarian Russian economy it is important to note that by 1916 women made up 72 per cent of the labour on peasant farms and 58 per cent on land-owners' estates.[6] There is evidence that the social abyss between the upper and lower classes in Russia was reflected in women's labour, as the women workers in industry were almost exclusively working-class, and upper-class women restricted themselves to hospital and charity work. In fact, the leading feminist journal, *Zhenskoe delo*, actively opposed the recruitment of women into industry.[7] However, the chief impact of the war on working-class women was to drive them to desperate measures to avoid the consequences of defeat. Women refugees were forced to turn to prostitution; children were abandoned to allow women to go to work, and theft and food rioting became common experiences for women trying to sustain their families.

It was not perhaps surprising therefore that the riot that became a revolution in Petrograd in February 1917 should have begun on International Women's Day.

In Britain, 4,808,000 women were in employment by the end of the war, an increase of over one and a half million. The exclusion of women from heavy industry and skilled work, such as shipbuilding and iron and steel, and from professions such as dentistry, accountancy and architecture, remained essentially unchanged in 1918. However, women did enter the civil service, transport areas, munitions factories, the post office and banking. In commerce and the civil service, women achieved lasting gains; however, no more than 5 per cent of new women workers were in these areas. Despite press stories about the classes mixing on the factory floor, most munitions workers were working class. Any middle-class women employed in factories usually appear to have acted as supervisors. Outside munitions, most of industry remained unenthusiastic about employing women workers, arguing that they were unwilling to take responsibility, unreliable and difficult to train. In mining and ship-building, employers and unions conspired to keep women out of the workforce, while in transport, where 555 per cent more women were employed, train-driving remained an exclusively male occupation. In this way, it is inaccurate to write of women 'taking over' from men. Attitudes that they were a cheap, temporary and unskilled workforce appear not to have altered in the war, and the lower pay rates for women reflected this attitude. Furthermore, the lack of adequate childcare arrangements meant that many of these new workers were single women. Lack of adequate training and the failure to alter the relationships between the male trade unions and the employers meant that women were not able to keep the jobs specifically labelled 'war work', and the attitude of the press changed dramatically, once the war ended. Women were urged to go back to the home, to domestic service and the laundry trade, and to release their jobs to the returning soldiers. Those women who refused to accept domestic service jobs from labour exchanges found their benefits stopped. The Restoration of Pre-War Practices Bill took jobs away from working-class women, while middle-class women benefited from the Sex Discrimination Removals Acts, which applied to the professions.

The First World War was not accompanied by any spectacular increase in women's work in Germany, as recent research has found that there was no noticeable above-average rise in female employment, either overall or in any particular industry in Germany.[8] In the munitions industry, employers preferred to seek military deferments for their skilled workers, or, if this failed, to employ foreigners and prisoners of war who could be paid less and treated worse than German women. The bulk of female munitions workers had formerly been factory workers or domestic servants and these workers had few illusions that, after the war, they would continue to have work in these areas. Sixty per cent confessed in 1917 that they didn't know what they would do after the war was over. Those women who were forced into paid employment by the pressures of the wartime economy entered industry on their own terms; they often resorted to home work, such as the production of military uniforms, sandbags, tent squares and biscuit-bags, which allowed them to continue to fulfil their family obligations. War did not usher in an excessive growth in female employment in Germany, but again a shift in patterns of employment was seen, away from domestic service, as 400,000 women left servitude during the war, never to return. The German government recognised the important role of women in providing for their families, especially after the collapse of the domestic consumer goods market, and actually set up a system of benefits, which, while very small, could at least be controlled by the woman in the home herself. In this way, the German government actually hindered their own attempts to mobilise the female workforce by allowing them to stay at home. Most women who had taken over traditionally male positions were made redundant as soon as the war ended.

The new women workers of the First World War were older than the pre-war average and likely to be married – most of these had gone from the home to the workshop. In 1914, half the single women recruited to industry had already had paid employment. On the issue of equal pay, the gap between male and female workers' wages in France narrowed during the war. In the traditionally poorly paid home-clothing trade, a minimum wage act of 1915 substantially increased female salaries. By 1917, an experienced 'munitionette' earned twice as much as a woman in the clothing trade. After strikes and disturbances in 1917, women workers were granted at least one day off per week. The British trade union leader, Mary Macarthur, led the campaign to protect the women forced to work in the munitions industry. She pointed out that women in the industry received on average less than half of what the men were paid. After much discussion it was agreed to increase women's wage-rates in the munitions industry. However, by 1918, whereas the average male wage in the munitions industry was £4 6s. 6d., for women it was only £2 2s. 4d.

There is further evidence of women becoming 'radicalised' during the war, as a result of their experience in the factories. In Germany, food riots and spontaneous strikes that the official unions were powerless to stop were, in the words of a police report, 'composed primarily of women'.[9] Women in France typically were in the vanguard of the strike movement (although the long-standing threat to conscript strikers may have made men less inclined to be seen agitating). Similarly, in Britain, women became much more active in union matters, with 383 trade unions with women members and 36 women-only unions by 1918.[10] In August 1918, women transport workers in London struck over 'equal pay' and their right, like their male colleagues, to a 'war bonus'. The employers conceded the latter but not the principle of 'equal pay'.

Male commentators were right in pointing to the fact that the war efforts required the mobilisation of women in the labour force. But they both understated the level of women's industrial work in the pre-war period and overstated the change caused by the war, partly because munitions work dominated the attention of observers and obscured the continuities and long-term aspects of the changes elsewhere. Women were recruited not from those previously unoccupied, but rather from those who had already been engaged in paid labour elsewhere in the economy. It is therefore inaccurate to describe the war as having had a 'revolutionary' effect on women's work; rather women's work, on buses, in factories or in hospitals, became more visible than it had been prior to 1914. The basic relationship between men and women did not change, and women continued to be expected to act as child-bearer, -carer and -rearer, as demonstrated by the wartime promotion of fertility by all the European governments to replace the losses in the national population. While millions of women were officially in work, the vast majority stayed at home during the Great War.

It is much more difficult to be precise about what war work meant to these women. Many upper- and middle-class women remember the social aspects of escaping the home and the pleasure in learning new skills. Others remember long hours and the burden of combining paid work, unpaid housework and child-minding, which included queuing for scarce supplies either before or after working hours. Undoubtedly, working in new situations and taking an active role in supporting the national war effort did raise the consciousness of many women and made them more aware of their own potential and more willing to speak out for their rights. But in many ways the war reinforced women's position in the home, for, as mothers, they had responsibilities which became more demanding as the war went on. Many households had to produce food rather than simply buying it. 'Making do' with whatever resources were available naturally placed a heavier burden on women than before the war, and this experience, unpaid, and often unappreciated, was a more common shared experience of women's war than the 'liberating' experience of labour.

Questions

1. Did women's war work actually reinforce traditional gender roles?
2. To what extent was the profile of women's work altered by the disruption of the First World War?

ANALYSIS (2): TO WHAT EXTENT DID THE WAR ADVANCE THE CAUSE OF WOMEN'S SUFFRAGE IN THE GREAT POWERS?

It was until quite recently accepted that the Great War acted as a significant breakthrough in the campaign for female suffrage. Women in Britain, Hungary, the United States, Germany and Russia were granted the right to vote during the war, and in France the Senate blocked it only after the Chamber of Deputies passed it by an overwhelming majority. However, certain points need to be borne in mind before such a simple analysis is accepted. First, in Germany and Russia, female suffrage was only granted after revolution had swept aside the entire edifice of Imperial government. It is certainly not valid to assert that women's right to vote was a matter of primary importance to the masses who brought down these regimes. Therefore, female suffrage was only indirectly caused by the war, as the war caused the revolutions which gave the feminists their opportunity. Second, in all the countries, male political leaders assented to the granting of the vote for women on their own terms, to suit their purposes, not those of the feminists, at this particular time. Third, the campaign for women's suffrage had a long history in the Western hemisphere before 1914, and several countries had conceded women's rights to vote by that date, such as New Zealand, Australia, Norway and Finland; and in Britain, women had equal voting rights to men in local elections. One must therefore recognise that the granting of the vote in three of the four powers during the Great War must be seen as part of a long-term international movement towards equalising the suffrage, as well as part of a wider campaign to widen the right to vote to include more men as well.

Two days after England declared war on Germany and after it participated in the great Peace Meeting in London, the National Union of Women's Suffrage Societies (NUWSS) announced that it was suspending all political activity until the war was over. On 7 August the Home Secretary announced that all suffragettes would be released from prison. In return, the Women's Social and Political Union (WSPU) agreed to end their militant activities and help the war effort. Some leaders of the

WSPU, such as Emmeline Pankhurst and her daughter Christabel, played an important role as speakers at meetings to recruit young men into the army, and the WSPU journal, the *Suffragette* was replaced by *Britannia*, which zealously hounded alleged traitors and called for the internment of enemy aliens and conscientious objectors. Encouraged by Lloyd George, anxious to recruit women munitions workers, Mrs Pankhurst encouraged a mass march of 20,000 women demanding the 'right to serve' on 7 July 1915. In contrast, Christabel's sister, Sylvia Pankhurst, was opposed to the war and, within her tiny East London Federation of Suffragettes (ELFS), vigorously campaigned for workers' rights, eventually advocating the establishment of British soviets in emulation of the Bolsheviks. Some members of the WSPU disagreed with the decision to call off militant activities. For example, Kitty Marion was so angry she went to the USA to help American women in their fight for the vote, and, in Britain, two groups split from the WSPU, the Suffragettes of the WSPU (SWSPU) and the Independent WSPU (IWSPU).[11] The NUWSS suffered for its support for the war as well, when eleven leading left-wing members who advocated a Women's International League for Peace and Freedom, resigned in April 1915.

While the outbreak of hostilities in 1914 led to fissures within the various suffrage organisations, it cannot be said that the campaign for women's suffrage came to a halt. The NUWSS continued to hold meetings, draft petitions and stage demonstrations in support of female suffrage. The war years also witnessed the removal of 'the main obstacles to reform . . . the WSPU abandoned militancy; Asquith resigned as prime minister in 1916; and the formation of a coalition government removed the issue from overt party politics'.[12] The women's suffrage clause in the Representation of the People Bill of 1918 reflected significant compromises worked out between the Conservative-dominated coalition government and the NUWSS during the war years. The legislation did not extend the franchise to women on equal terms with men: women had to be aged 30 or above and local government electors or the wives of such electors; men only had to be aged 21 or above or military veterans aged 19 or above. Women who had served their country as munitions workers and who were typically under 30 and unmarried were not enfranchised by the measure. Thus, there is little evidence for some historians' contention that suffrage was conceded as a reward for women's contribution to the war effort. The women who gained the vote in 1918 were more likely to be married, to have children, and to have no interest in a career which brought with it further demands for equality. Conservatives and right-wing Liberals felt there would be little threat to the existing political order from such new voters and, in light of political behaviour after the war, they seem to have made quite a shrewd judgement.

In France it was 'widely expected . . . to introduce the female suffrage'.[13] Some, such as the socialist deputy, Bracke, believed that all the arguments against women's suffrage had collapsed in the face of their achievements in the war. Even those traditionally opposed to the idea conceded that war widows and relations of fallen soldiers should be granted the right to vote. In May 1919, therefore, when the Chamber of Deputies debated the issue, hopes were high. The former Prime Minister, Viviani cited the examples of other countries who were granting political rights to women and called for immediate equality in the French constitution. The chamber passed the bill by 344 to 97. The Senate, however, failed to discuss the bill until 1922 and then threw it out by 156 votes to 134. What were the reasons given for this move? As well as the traditional fears that the powers of the husband would be undermined, the Radical-Socialists believed that French Catholic women would vote for Catholic parties and threaten the secular authority of the republic. In a similar way, the right to vote in municipal elections was approved by the Chamber but defeated in the Senate in 1927. This behaviour revealed, not any male chauvinism on the part of the French population, but rather the insecure attitude of the Third Republic's political establishment and the weakness of the feminist movement itself. The women of France had to await the downfall of the Third Republic itself before they gained the vote in 1945.

By contrast, in Russia, the feminist movement achieved its goal of female emancipation, at least temporarily. Russian feminists, though relatively few in number, had organised a League of Equal Rights before the war and had presented a bill giving women equal voting rights in state elections to the Duma in 1912. The coming of the war overwhelmed the organisations that existed, however, and most feminists found their time taken up with war work. One such body, the Women's Economic Union, created a workers' restaurant, but failed to achieve its objective of establishing lectures and a workshop in imitation of Sylvia Pankhurst's ELFS. Feminists did not, as far as we are able to tell, participate in the demonstrations and strikes which led to the downfall of the Tsar in February 1917. Once the Imperial Government had fallen, however, feminists grasped the opportunity that it presented. The Provisional Government issued a programme promising political and civil rights, but did nothing for the women's movement. The League of Equal Rights immediately began a propaganda campaign to demand the vote, and on 18 July a procession of 40,000 women marched on the Tauride Palace to lobby the Soviet and the Duma. There they received

Rodzianko's support and, two days later, the Prime Minister, Lvov, promised to include women in the new electoral system. Having only just defeated an attempted Bolshevik coup in the July Days, and facing a possible right-wing assault from leading army generals, the Provisional Government needed as much support as it could muster. Consequently, men with no particular enthusiasm for female suffrage quickly acceded to the feminists' demands; as Lvov put it, 'why shouldn't women vote? I don't see what's the problem.'[14] The feminists reciprocated by continuing to support the Provisional Government and the Russian war effort, supporting the formation of women's battalions and calling for a general labour conscription of women. Most feminists attacked the Bolsheviks for their peace policy and 'coarse material incentives'. Therefore, with the Bolshevik coup in October, their journals and organisations were swiftly closed. Feminism as a separate force ceased to exist in Russia and the demand for the vote became irrelevant after the forcible closing of the Constituent Assembly in January 1918.

In a similar fashion in Germany, the vote was granted to women as part of the German 'Revolution' of 1918–19. At first, in co-operation with the Ministry of the Interior, the Federation of German Women's Organisations (*Bund Deutscher Frauenverein* – BDF) set up a 'National Women's Service', which set up soup kitchens and hospital wards and looked after orphans and the homeless. Until Easter 1917, feminist activity was abandoned in the hope that support of the war effort would bring the women's movement concessions after the war. The Kaiser's 'Easter Message' in 1917 changed this position, however, as it promised greater public participation in politics once the war was won. Nothing was said about the rights of women, and the Conservative and Catholic Centre Parties voiced their opposition to female suffrage on principle. The BDF therefore launched a campaign to win the vote, despite internal opposition from conservative women's groups, and used its influence to persuade local branches of the Progressive Party to endorse it. The leadership of the Progressives and all other parties, except the SPD and USPD, failed to support the cause though, and it seemed, in early 1918, that the experience of war had done little to improve the chances of women gaining the vote in Germany. With the acceptance of defeat by Hindenburg and Ludendorff in September 1918, however, the situation changed. Prince Max's moderate reform proposals contained no mention of female suffrage, but when the Kiel sailors mutinied, they included women's political rights among their demands. Party leaders in Berlin continued to oppose such a suggestion, until Max resigned and handed power to the socialists, whose programme, announced on 12 November, included female suffrage. However, the socialists' motive for introducing votes for women was primarily to win votes, as they were aware of their limited popular support, rather than any commitment to feminist causes. As Richard Evans comments, 'the survival of the institutional basis of the Empire would make it very difficult for women to gain equal rights in other spheres, despite their possession of the vote'.[15]

In this way, it seems that the causes of the enfranchisement of women in the three Great Powers are similar. In Britain, Russia and Germany, wartime circumstances dictated that the voting rights of *men* had to be reformed. In Russia and Germany, these circumstances were the overthrow of an autocratic system of government; in Britain, the disruption of war had made the previous electoral system unworkable. Women campaigners took advantage of the debates on the type of franchise reform to be introduced to press for their demands, on the grounds of their pre-war arguments as well as the justification of women's wartime service. Also, certain male politicians in all three countries felt that they would gain political advantage for themselves by doing so, as long as they determined what form that reform would take. In France, the lack of a well-established and intellectually respectable campaign for women's votes before the war, and lack of reform of the established Third Republic's franchise, meant that French women lacked the opportunity, as well as the organisation, of their counterparts in the other countries.

Questions

1. Was the vote granted by three of the Great Powers due to external events rather than the actions of the feminist bodies themselves?
2. How important was women's wartime service in altering male perceptions of their political role?

SOURCES

1. SOCIAL CHANGE

Source A: from 'Women's War Work' by Lady Randolph Churchill, 1915.

Truly, where dress is concerned, the change of feeling is immense. It is difficult to realise that the pretty business girl, who, seated in train or tube, steadily knits her way to town in the morning and back again at night, is the gay butterfly who less than two years ago was contemptuously reported to 'put all her salary on her back'.

Source B: from 'The War in its Effect upon Women' by Helena Swanwick, 1916.

When a great naval engagement took place, the front page of a progressive daily paper was taken up with portraits of the officers and men who had won distinction, and the back page with portraits of simpering mannequins in extravagantly fashionable hats; not frank advertisement, mind you, but exploitation of women under the guise of news supposed to be peculiarly interesting to the feeble-minded creatures. When a snapshot was published of the first women ticket collectors in England, the legend underneath the picture ran 'Superwomen'! It took the life and death of Edith Cavell to open the eyes of the Prime Minister to the fact that there were thousands of women giving life and service to their country.

Source C: Mary Macarthur, a trade unionist, writing in 1918.

Of all the changes wrought by the war, none has been greater than the change in the status and position of women, but it is not so much that woman herself has changed but that man's perception of her has changed.

Source D: from 'Women's Work – Ersatz Men's Work?' by Magda Trott, 1915.

Even on the first day it was noticeable that not everything would proceed as had been supposed. Male colleagues looked askance at the 'intruder' who dared to usurp the position and bread of a colleague now fighting for the Fatherland, and who would, it was fervently hoped, return in good health. Moreover, the lady who came as a substitute received exactly half of the salary of the gentleman colleague who had previously occupied the same position. A dangerous implication, since if the lady made good, the boss might continue to draw on female personnel; the saving on salaries would clearly be substantial. It became essential to use all means to show the boss that female help was no substitute for men's work, and a united male front was organised.

Source E: from *The Woman Worker*, March 1916.

According to Mr Lloyd George, never were there such useful workers as women munitions workers. Well, it is very nice to be praised by so important a man and it is even nicer that he should take the trouble to have a book filled with the pictures of the girls at work. We women, however, have always had in our minds a lurking suspicion that we were, after all, as clever as the men, and it is pleasant enough to hear Mr Lloyd George say so. But there is a conclusion to be drawn from all this. If girls are as important and as clever as men then they are as valuable to the employer. If this is so it becomes a duty of the girls to see now and always that they receive the same pay as the men. Otherwise, all their cleverness and their intelligence go to helping the employer and bringing down the wages of their husbands, fathers and brothers.

Source F: Arthur Marwick, a historian, describes the impact of the war.

It was the war, in creating simultaneously a proliferation of Government committees and departments and a shortage of men, which brought a sudden and irreversible advance in the economic and social power of a category of women employees which extended from the sprigs of the aristocracy to the daughters of the proletariat.

Source G: a French historian offers a judgement.

The war probably did adjust some public attitudes, but one must also ask if this new mood was far-reaching or long-lasting. Many of the changes were temporary, enduring only as long as the unusual circumstances which produced them. It is more accurate to see the war as only one factor in a longer and slower evolution than as a momentous change.

Source H: Deborah Thom, a modern historian.

The change in the working woman's perception of herself and her capacity to organise in defence of her interests was not fully recognised until the war but in fact that change was revealed, and diverted and delayed, by war rather than created by it. Mrs Fawcett still saw women in industry with nineteenth century spectacles when she wrote in 1918, 'The war revolutionised the industrial position of women. It found them serfs and left them free.'

Questions

1. Who was 'Edith Cavell' (Source B)? (2 marks)
2. How far does Source A support Source B's criticisms of how women were perceived at the beginning of the war? (4 marks)
*3. How far is the assertion in Source C borne out by the evidence contained in Sources D and E? (5 marks)
4. Compare and contrast the judgements of the historians in Sources F, G and H. (6 marks)
5. In light of the Sources and your own knowledge, would you agree that any transformation in women's social position during the Great War was exaggerated by contemporary feminists, journalists and politicians to serve their own purposes? (8 marks)

Worked answer

*3. [To avoid a full answer to a question such as this becoming excessively long and time-consuming, it is important that the answer is divided into two sections – those aspects of the first source that are supported by the others, and those aspects that aren't. It is not necessary to try to explain why the sources do or do not support each other.]

In Source C, Mary Macarthur claims that women have not particularly changed during the war, rather 'that man's perception of her has changed'. In Source D, Magda Trott supports this view when she describes how male workers were forced to reappraise women, as they were introduced into factories in positions that had previously been exclusively held by men. Furthermore, in Source E, it is stated that Lloyd George, a senior political figure, had claimed that 'never were there such useful workers as women munitions workers' and that he had issued propaganda material to demonstrate the vital war work that women were carrying out. This demonstrates how male politicians' perceptions of women had been affected by the war and how this message was passed on to the public at large.

Both Sources D and E indicate that not all male perceptions had altered, however. Source D mentions the hostility faced by women, who, it was feared, would 'usurp' male workers, demonstrating the persistent attitude that women should not work and that men should be able to support their whole family on their wages. Both D and E also refer to the unequal pay that women received, which shows that women workers were still regarded less highly than men and treated as unskilled workers. However, Macarthur did not claim in Source C that men now perceived women as equals, rather that their perception had changed. It seems that this was the case, but that the perception was not necessarily one of approval.

SOURCES

2. THE RIGHT TO VOTE

Source I: Millicent Fawcett in a speech to the NUWSS at the beginning of the war.

Women, your country needs you ... let us show ourselves worthy of citizenship, whether our claim to it be recognised or not.

Source J: from 'The War in its Effect upon Women' by Helena Swanwick, 1916.

What the war has put in a fresh light, so that even the dullest can see, is that if the State may claim women's lives and those of their sons and husbands and lovers, if it may absorb all private and individual life, as at present, then indeed the condition of those who have no voice in the State is a condition of slavery, and Englishmen don't feel quite happy at the thought that their women are still slaves, while their Government is saying that they are waging a war of liberation. Many women had long ago become acutely aware of their ignominious position, but the jolt of war has made many more aware of it.

Source K: Sebastien Schlittenbauer, leader of the Centre Party in the Bavarian Landtag, writing in 1918.

In the long run, it will no longer do that our German girls receive absolutely no political-civic instruction in school, and in the long run, it will no longer do that we exclude women so totally from political life. How shall the woman have an understanding of state emergencies in the hour of danger, if, in the hours of peace, she is never trusted with the spirit and essence of the state. I emphatically support the right of women to vote.

Source L: from a speech by the Russian feminist Shishkina-Iavein, following the February Revolution.

We have come here to remind you that women were your faithful comrades in the gigantic struggle for the freedom of the Russian people; that they also have been filling up the prisons, and boldly marching to the galleys. The best of us looked into the eyes of death without fear.

We declare that the Constituent Assembly in which only one half of the population will be represented can in no wise be regarded as expressing the will of the whole people, but only half of it.

We want no more promises of good will. We have had enough of them! We demand an official and clear answer – that women will have votes in the Constituent Assembly.

Source M: from the liberal newspaper *The Nation*, 27 May 1916.

[Women's] qualities hidden and diffused in time of peace, have suddenly been concentrated and illuminated by our hour of need. Those who lacked the occasion or the insight to recognise them before, have been surprised into this general homage. We would not speak of the vote as a reward for all this service. We prefer to say that the nation has seen that it impoverishes its own life by a refusal to give full scope to all this ability and public spirit. We cannot afford to face the future with one-half of the nation's brains in shackles, with one of its hands still vainly reaching for its tool.

Source N: from the Berard Report on women's suffrage in France, 1919.

The Catholic mentality of the majority of French women, combined with the hostility of the church towards the republic and liberty, means that women's suffrage would lead to clerical reaction.

Women are different creatures than men, filled with sentiment and tears rather than hard political reason: their hands are not for political pugilism or holding ballots, but for kisses.

Questions

1. What was the 'NUWSS' (Source I)? (2 marks)
2. What does Source I reveal about the suffragists' motives during the First World War? (4 marks)
3. How similar are the justifications for granting women the vote given in Sources J, K and L? (6 marks)
4. Compare the attitudes towards women's involvement in national politics given in Sources M and N. (5 marks)
*5. After reading the Sources and in light of your own knowledge, would you agree that women's suffrage was an 'accidental consequence of the First World War'? (8 marks)

Worked answer

*5. [Many students think it is always best to 'sit on the fence' when asked a direct question like this – I disagree – it is much better to present evidence to support either side of the argument, and then to come to a conclusion in which you reiterate the crucial evidence which has led you to come down on one side. Naturally, this depends on you having done enough revision to be able to make an independent judgement – but that is, after all, what every history exam requires.]

Most of the sources would seem to indicate that the war had a direct effect in causing the emancipation of women. Millicent Fawcett's call in Source I, for women to prove themselves 'worthy of citizenship' by war work, appears to have paid dividends, for the 'ability and public spirit' (Source M) which women had demonstrated have been recognised and rewarded. After the war, it was unthinkable that 'women are still slaves' (Source J), and men should 'no longer . . . exclude women . . . from political life' (Source K). It was widely felt by suffrage campaigners throughout Europe that the pre-war arguments that women did not deserve the vote because they played no active role in the defence of the state had been disproved by a 'total war' which had seen women working in munitions factories, replacing male workers who had gone to the Front and even forming military units.

On the other hand, Source J seems to suggest that the nature of the war, as 'a war of liberation', rather than women's contribution, made equalising political rights a necessity. Likewise, Source K, in wanting women to have influence over the 'spirit and essence of the state', does so to strengthen Germany, as her present system of government had brought the country to the edge of defeat by 1918, not to reward women. In Source L, Russian feminists convinced Provisional Government representatives of their right to vote by their actions opposing the tsarist government 'in the gigantic struggle for the freedom of the Russian people', rather than any war work.

The argument that the war was an 'accident' which disrupted some states to such a degree that wide-ranging political reform was unavoidable, seems confirmed by the case of France. Here women had taken an unprecedented role in industry during the war, making up 46 per cent of France's workforce by 1918, yet demands for the vote were denied, because traditional fears of women's 'Catholic mentality' (Source N) asserted themselves and the need for considerable political reform was absent. Women had not proved themselves more fit to vote in any other countries; rather female suffrage was granted to suit the politicians who had come to power during the war in those countries, and was therefore an 'accidental' consequence of the war.

5

THE CHANGING ROLE OF GOVERNMENT

BACKGROUND NARRATIVE

The longer the First World War dragged on, the more the new-found political unity that had been so loudly proclaimed in all the Great Powers, the 'spirit of August 1914', gradually came under pressure, as no government was able to achieve a swift success despite the confident picture maintained by the press. Every government recruited military and civilian personnel on a huge scale, from sections of the population never previously involved, even indirectly, in combat, and flung men and ordnance against the enemy in huge battles, which left every European state close to bankruptcy. They increasingly, albeit reluctantly, intervened in the economy and assumed vast powers over their population in order to ensure the redoubling of the war effort. The British government had, through the Defence of the Realm Act, granted itself enormous directive powers which laid the basis for extensive government interference. The first Act, of August 1914, gave the Cabinet the power to 'issue regulations as to the powers and duties of the Admiralty and Army Council, and other persons acting on their behalf, for securing the public safety and defence of the realm'. In France, a 'state of siege' was declared by President Poincaré, which placed eight departments under the control of the Commander in Chief, Joffre, and subject to military law. By September, this had increased to 33 departments and the army was given the power to try civilians. Under the terms of the Prussian Law of Siege, executive power devolved onto the Deputy Commanding Generals of Germany's 24 military districts upon the declaration of a state of national emergency. This authority included censorship, the organisation of transportation and the preservation of public order. The Russian government, meanwhile, exploited the political truce of 1914 to employ the full force of the Tsar's autocratic powers. Yet, despite this, victory still seemed a distant hope, except in the minds of optimistic, ambitious generals. Unsurprisingly, therefore, the initial political unity came under strain as the tactics, personalities, commitment and competence of the leading political figures of Europe were questioned by public and opponents alike.

Following the disastrous failure in 1915 of the Gallipoli campaign to outflank the Central Powers, the French and the British landed troops at Salonika in Greece in order to bring aid to the Serbs, but the campaign was once again a total fiasco. Bulgaria promptly joined the war on Germany's side, while the Greeks announced they would remain neutral. French and British troops advanced into Serbia, but were insufficient to prevent her defeat and were forced back to Salonika.

Throughout 1915, the Western Front remained deadlocked, but in 1916, the Germans attempted to turn the war decisively in their favour, when they attacked the exposed French fortress at Verdun. A planned British offensive was brought forward to take pressure off the French, and on 1 July 1916, the largest and most bloody military campaign of the war to date was launched on a front 30 miles north and south of the River Somme. Despite their successes in the Balkans and their ability to withstand the Allied attacks, the Germans began running short of supplies, especially food. In desperation to break the stalemate they embarked upon two reckless moves. First, in 1917, they relaunched their campaign of unrestricted submarine warfare, which threatened every merchant ship, neutral or enemy, in the waters around Britain. As the previous submarine campaign had culminated in the sinking of the Lusitania and the death of 139 Americans in 1915, it was inevitable that such a course of action would lead to further American deaths. Second, the foreign minister, Zimmerman, sent a telegram to the Mexican government offering support for Mexican claims to US territory if they declared war on the USA. This was intercepted by the British and passed on to President Woodrow

Wilson. These actions led to the entry of the USA on the side of the Entente, with its massive human and economic resources, which the Central Powers could not hope to match.

ANALYSIS (1): WHY DID THE WAR LEAD TO THE FALL OF ALL THE GOVERNMENTS OF 1914?

For all four Great Powers, the early years of the war brought the effective fall of the governments that had declared war in 1914. These political crises were ultimately caused by the costly failures of the military campaigns of 1915 and 1916, and all involved a struggle for authority between politicians and generals, a battle which was resolved differently from state to state.

The survival of Goremykin's administration in Russia, despite the disasters of the opening months of the war, is a testament to the Tsar's disdain for public sentiment and the lack of popular influence over the government. The execution for spying of Colonel Miasoyedov had cast a shadow of suspicion over his patron, Sukhomlinov, the War Minister. Sukhomlinov was dismissed, arrested, tried and imprisoned for treason. However, this and the loss of Russian Poland, together with the German background of Tsarina Alexandra and other Russian nobles, led many to draw wild conclusions of treason at the highest levels. To stem this loss of trust, the reactionary Minister of the Interior, Maklakov, was also dismissed, along with the Minister of Justice, and the Tsar recalled the Duma on 19 July 1915. However, when the Duma reconvened, critics argued that 'the entire administrative structure of Russia must be reformed',[1] and demanded 'a government having the confidence of the country behind it',[2] representing all the major parties. A 'Progressive Bloc', led by Prince Lvov, was formed, encompassing three-quarters of Duma and State Council members. The Bloc's programme demanded only limited reforms and a united cabinet that would co-operate with the Duma, and ten members of the Tsar's government, including the new Minister of War, Polivanov, urged him to compromise. It was, therefore, both brave and foolish of the Tsar to dismiss Grand Duke Nikolai in August and assume personal command of the army on 22 August: brave, because he demonstrated thus his personal commitment to Russia's war effort; foolish, because he would bear the blame for any subsequent failures of the Russian army, and because he left the command of the domestic situation to his wife. Rodzianko, the President of the Duma, and the dissident ministers wrote to the Tsar, begging him to reverse this action. However Goremykin urged Nicholas to sack the reformist ministers, and Alexandra supported him, saying that they 'needed smacking'.[3] Nicholas prorogued the Duma and announced full confidence in his Prime Minister, prompting Sazonov, the Foreign Minister, to exclaim, 'That old man [Goremykin] is utterly mad!' Over the next months, he and the other dissident ministers were sacked. Only in Russia was the government effectively dismissed for wanting to execute the war more efficiently and in keeping with the wishes of the public.

In Britain, Asquith's Liberal government, in office since the General Election of 1910, remained in power for only nine months after the outbreak of war. The army's failure to achieve a breakthrough in early 1915 was blamed on the government by Sir John French, who cited an inadequate supply of munitions. The Unionist Business Committee was quick to exploit this, putting down a motion on the issue in the House of Commons. The pressure on Asquith increased in May 1915 when Sir John Fisher, the First Sea Lord, resigned in protest at the decision to send more ships to Gallipoli after the failure of the initial attack. The Conservative leader, Andrew Bonar Law, had not intended to bring the Liberal government down, but he saw no way to resolve this crisis without a change of personnel. Lloyd George agreed: 'Of course we must have a coalition, for the alternative is impossible' – referring to the impossibility of organising a general election during wartime. Asquith accepted a deal with the Conservatives, hoping that they would bear the responsibility for sacking the popular Kitchener, who was blamed for the shell shortage (he was perfectly willing to demote Churchill, who was blamed for the Gallipoli disaster). Kitchener actually survived, but lost his powers over supply to Lloyd George's new Ministry of Munitions. The Conservatives received little reward for their support (Bonar Law became Colonial Secretary and Balfour replaced Churchill at the Admiralty), which angered Conservative backbenchers, who believed that Asquith had deceived them, especially when Labour received their first ministerial post in the coalition.

However, government continued to function much as before, presiding over more military disasters, which culminated in the long-drawn-out agony of the Somme in 1916, and hampered by Liberal opposition to increased government control in areas such as conscription. The press, especially *The Times*, continued to castigate Asquith for his shortcomings as a war leader. Eventually Bonar Law, aware of rumblings of discontent from within his party, demanded that a small War Cabinet should be empowered to make all vital decisions. He was supported in this by Lloyd George, who had become War Minister in July 1916 following Kitchener's death, and who felt frustrated by his lack of control over the military establishment. Asquith, hoping to outmanouevre his critics, resigned in December 1916, but found himself replaced when Lloyd George patched together a deal which saw him, a Liberal, become Prime Minister of a predominantly Conservative coalition, when the rest of the Liberal ministers resigned. The War Cabinet comprised Lloyd George, Bonar Law, Lord Curzon, Alfred Milner and the Labour leader, Arthur Henderson. The ambition of the Conservatives in general and Lloyd George in particular – combined with the popular perception of Asquith as an unsuitable war-leader, reinforced by anti-Liberal elements of the press – thus radically altered the complexion of British politics and would fatally divide the Liberals.

The French Chamber of Deputies, having delegated vast powers to the government and proclaimed the 'Union Sacrée' on 4 August 1914, adjourned indefinitely. However, the first challenge to the 'Union' came on 26 August when Viviani, without consulting Parliament, excluded the Radical, Joseph Caillaux, due to his pacifist views. A second blow fell when Georges Clemenceau refused to serve in the government. As a result, Viviani's Cabinet was composed of less prominent figures such as Ribot, Delcassé and Briand. Protests were interrupted by the threat to Paris in September and the flight of the government and deputies to Bordeaux until December. This left the military controlling affairs, so it was unsurprising that hostility towards the government initially came from deputies who resented the almost dictatorial control over affairs exercised by General Headquarters, commanded by General Joffre. The press, notably Clemenceau's journal *L'Homme Libre*, was influential in fostering criticism of the government. Indeed, *L'Homme Libre* was closed down by the government censor, only to reappear under the ironic title, *L'Homme Enchaîné*.

At the next session of the chamber in December 1914, the Union held, and budget credits were voted, but as deputies who had seen action at the Front returned with information on munitions shortages and poor medical services, the political truce became harder to maintain. Millerand, the Minister of War, was the first target of attack. Parliamentary commissions, operating in secret so as not to damage morale, uncovered serious deficiencies in planning, especially in the crucial area of artillery, and the chief of the artillery section, General Baquet was replaced by a politician, Albert Thomas in May 1915. Viviani's government suffered further criticism for its poor economic management, as agricultural production fell and unemployment remained at over 30 per cent. The failure of France's four western military offensives of 1915 led to growing pressure from the press and the left wing. The Salonika campaign, equally disastrous, left Viviani hopelessly exposed, as he was closely associated with the expedition's commander, General Sarrail. As numerous parliamentary commissions demanded changes, Viviani complained to President Poincaré that 'I can no longer keep going. I spend three or four hours every day with the commissions.'[4] Viviani eventually resigned in October 1915, and Aristide Briand, a veteran socialist, became Prime Minister, aiming to revitalise the war effort and increase the power of politicians at the expense of the generals. To this end, Millerand was replaced by Galliéni, who immediately challenged Joffre's direction of the war. In France, where frequent changes of government were the pre-war norm, the political crisis there had the least impact on the direction of government policy.

In Germany, the Social Democrats quickly felt deceived by the 'Burgfriede' when Bethmann-Hollweg's 'September Programme' revealed plans for an annexationist peace. However, they could do little, under the Bismarckian constitution, to challenge the government. In fact the greatest threat to Bethmann-Hollweg came from the military. In 1916, he successfully obstructed the demands of the Chief of Staff, Falkenhayn, to relaunch unrestricted submarine warfare, but this led to the resignation in protest of Tirpitz. Falkenhayn continued to argue that only submarine warfare could defeat Britain, and after Romania's declaration of war on Austria-Hungary and the failure of the attempt to 'bleed France white' at Verdun, Bethmann-Hollweg persuaded the Kaiser to dismiss him, appointing Paul Von Hindenburg as Chief of Staff, with Erich von Ludendorff as his deputy in August 1916. The chancellor possibly hoped that the popularity of these two men, idolised for their successes on the Eastern Front, could persuade the German Right to accept a negotiated peace, but he reckoned without their ambition, especially Ludendorff's. Once Romania had been defeated, the High Command (*Oberste Heeresleitung* – OHL) insisted that the unrestricted submarine warfare campaign be restarted. The threat of US intervention was dismissed by the chief of naval staff, Holtzendorff, who offered his 'word of honour' that no American soldier would set foot in France. When Bethmann-Hollweg continued to express reluctance, Ludendorff threatened his and Hindenburg's resignations, a favourite tactic. The Kaiser and the chancellor knew that German morale would not withstand the loss of these two, so, on 9 January 1917, Bethmann-Hollweg backed down, staying on as chancellor out of duty to the Kaiser and to prevent Germany's allies and enemies perceiving a conflict in the government. Although he struggled on, disliked by the military due to his failure to control the Reichstag, and distrusted by the Reichstag because of his failure to secure peace, Bethmann-Hollweg's authority was virtually destroyed by the affair. This marked the effective start of Hindenburg and Ludendorff's 'silent dictatorship'.

With the USA's declaration of war, food shortages worsening, the U-boat campaign failing, and the example of the February Revolution in Russia, the government sought, in the Kaiser's annual Easter message of 1917, to mollify the workers with promises of 'the extension of our political, economic and social life, as soon as the state of war allows', with particular emphasis placed on the reform of the unequal Prussian franchise. Although it infuriated Ludendorff, who called it a 'kow-tow to the Russian revolution', it was not enough. Widespread food riots, strikes and even a hunger strike on the ship *Prince Regent Leopold* in April drove the Reichstag into open opposition. In July, a leading Centre Party politician, Matthias Erzberger, after seeing the poor state of the army on the Eastern Front, declared submarine warfare a failure and demanded an 'immediate peace of reconciliation'. The Reichstag passed his 'Peace Resolution' by 212 votes to 126 on 19 July. The furious OHL forced Bethmann-Hollweg to resign, replacing him with Georg Michaelis, an administrator at the Prussian food office, described by one SPD deputy as 'the fairy angel, tied to the Christmas tree for the children's benefit'. Hereafter, the OHL directed the war effort, taking every imaginable risk to internal social order simply to keep the war going, seemingly unaware that public support for the war was slipping away.

The failure to achieve the expected swift victory weakened confidence in every European government. As 1915 confirmed that no country had anticipated the huge social and economic scale of a protracted modern war, ministerial scalps were demanded by the press, the public and in some cases the military. In democratic Britain and France, this resulted in cabinet reshuffles, achieved with minimal disruption of public morale. In Russia it revealed the inadequacies both of the Tsar and the Russian constitution, as demands for greater efficiency were ignored. Most complex of all, in Germany the experience of stalemate drove the military into taking greater control of decision making, and the Reichstag into demanding a negotiated peace. As the chancellor could not satisfy the latter without offending the former, his position quickly became untenable as Bismarck's constitution began to unravel.

Questions

1. Were the governments of 1914 capable of efficiently waging 'total war'?
2. Does the First World War mark a watershed in the political history of all the Great Powers?

ANALYSIS (2): HOW FAR HAD THE GOVERNMENTS OF THE GREAT POWERS INCREASED THE POWER OF THE STATE OVER THEIR CITIZENS BY 1917?

The pressures of war forced every Great Power gradually to abandon *laissez-faire* principles of economics and government in favour of greater state intervention. Governments faced a difficult task – to fight a war, while simultaneously preserving living standards as far as possible so as not to suffer a fatal collapse of morale in the rear. As one French cartoonist put it – 'Let's hope the civilians can hold out.'[5] In order to achieve this, every state was increasingly forced to intervene directly in society and the economy.

DORA gave successive British governments virtually limitless powers over their citizens, even altering the passage of time in 1916, when British Summer Time was introduced, enabling firms to take advantage of longer, lighter evenings. The right to trial by jury was initially suspended, and even when reinstated in 1915, after protests in the House of Lords, it was still used in cases of 'military emergency' and to legitimise the court martial that sentenced the Irish Republicans responsible for the Easter Rising in 1916. Innumerable wartime restrictions were enforced, including a blackout in London, a prohibition on whistling for cabs and keeping racing pigeons or flying kites. In 1914, all pubs were limited to evening opening, and by the end of the year London pubs were forced to close at 10 p.m. The establishment of the Central Control Board (Liquor Traffic) in 1915 led to restricted opening hours in areas where important war work was being done, which ultimately extended to all but a few rural areas. This, and the wartime weakening of beer to preserve hops and grain, achieved one government objective – drunkenness significantly declined.

The government was less inclined to intervene in the food supply, and until late 1916 there was little need. During 1917, however, the government was forced, by strikes and demonstrations, to subsidise bread and potato prices and to create Divisional Food Commissions with the authority to introduce local rationing. In 1918, butter, margarine, lard, meat and sugar were all nationally rationed, and by the end of the war the government controlled 85 per cent of food sales, thereby restraining prices and preventing shortages. These restrictions were rigorously enforced with 65,000 prosecutions for breaches of the food control orders.

In August 1914, a Railway Executive Committee, comprising the ten general managers of the larger companies, assumed control of the railway network. Alongside this, all shipping in home waters was requisitioned, and, by 1918, the government controlled all maritime and canal transport. Other immediate controls included the suspension of stock-exchange dealing, restrictions on the printing of paper money and an export ban on explosives. Profits in government-controlled industries were fixed at 1913 levels. For the sake of public unity, the Munitions of War Act limited excess war profits of private companies to 20 per cent of pre-war profits which, although difficult to enforce because so many new firms were established during the war, created an impression of equality of sacrifice.

The explosion of regulatory roles adopted by the state led to multi-faceted intervention in the workplace – canteens, childcare, inspectors and government committees on health and nutrition, such as a Health of Munitions Workers Committee, set up in September 1915, 'to consider and advise on questions of industrial fatigue, hours of labour and other matters affecting personal health'. Rent restrictions were enacted in 1915 and, under Lloyd George, new departments such as Labour, Food, Pensions, Information and Air were established, with vast increases in the numbers of civil servants. By 1918 the Ministry of Munitions owned more than 250 factories, administering a further 20,000, and the government employed 5 million workers. A huge experiment in 'state capitalism' was under way, and the significance of this was not lost on workers, employers, unions and Labour politicians. The change in atti-tudes is aptly illustrated by Lloyd George's famous promise of 'habitations for the heroes who have won the war' the day after the armistice, and the subsequent establishment of the Ministry of Health.

In August 1914 the French state arrogated to itself the power to requisition factories and materials. It rarely did so, however, preferring to collaborate with industry rather than dictate to it. Exports of food and other vital commodities were banned and customs duties on food imports were lifted. Railways were brought under state control and were run by the military until March 1915, when they were systematically reorganised for efficiency. A decree of 15 July 1915 aimed at complete industrial mobilisation, making substantial government subsidies available to war industries. In October, the government assumed the power to requisition crops for feeding the civilian population. In 1916 the War Council placed a series of restrictions on food: 'national' bread replaced the traditional long baton, and ice cream and sweets (including chocolates) were banned. The government began ordering meatless days in Paris, pre-vented shops being lit by electricity or gas after 6 p.m. to save fuel, closed restaurants at 9.30 p.m. and made theatres, music-halls and cinemas shut on one night of the week (increasing to four by 1918). The following year, restaurants were forbidden to serve more than two dishes to a customer and sugar was rationed. Private houses were only allowed a single light bulb for each room. At the end of 1917, the government took over coal distribution, introducing rationing. Bread rationing followed shortly afterwards, but French food restrictions were never as stringently enforced as those in Britain – the rich could always eat well in restaurants. The German advance on Paris in spring 1918 saw a final flurry of government intervention. Schoolchildren were evacuated and rations were cut to a bare subsistence.

None the less, the market remained dominant. As Albert Thomas observed, 'the Ministry co-ordinates the public services; buyers, consumers and producers; and the private sector; scientists, industries, hydraulic power and manpower'.[6] Ultimately, industry could always close down production if it did not like the terms the state offered. The only way to guarantee production would be to requisition factories, but the ideological and practical obstacles to such a drastic step prevented the government from ever pursuing it. Indeed, although a socialist, Thomas consistently argued that private enterprise was the most effective means to achieve increased production. Taxation of war profits was poorly enforced, and many companies avoided payment or concealed the true extent of their gains. Thomas was more interventionist in fostering new processes, which the influx of unskilled labour necessitated. This required the modernisation of industry, and the state provided much of the requisite investment capital.

By contrast, the Minister of Commerce, Etienne Clementel, saw the war as an opportunity to modernise French industry and commerce for the post-war good of the economy, and favoured a greater degree of state intervention and direction. After Thomas's fall, Clementel created consortia to control the provision of industrial raw materials, maintaining quantity and quality of supply. Cotton was used as a guinea pig for this experiment, with a joint stock company being set up with 10 million francs capital to purchase necessary supplies, and other industries followed.

There were limits to state power in both France and Britain, however. Coercion was rarely employed against strikers and collective bargaining was introduced. Censorship was somewhat haphazard and free reporting of parliamentary proceedings ensured that protest did still have a voice. Even pacifism was largely tolerated despite a number of high-profile trials. The governments in both countries were well aware that the war was being fought against 'Militarism' and that any reliance on coercion would undermine the democratic appearance of the government. Persuasion was far more acceptable and both governments relied heavily upon private agencies to bolster public morale.

In Germany, the Reichstag delegated its legislative powers to the Prussian-dominated Bundesrat on 4 August. This chamber concerned itself chiefly with mobilising the economy for war, creating powerful agencies which were mostly housed within the Prussian War Ministry. However, this created another layer of authority, overlapping that of the Deputy Commanding Generals. It was unsurprising therefore that public power intruded on private life to an unprecedented degree and could be at times unsystematic, contradictory and unfair. Within weeks of war breaking out, city authorities and other local governments fixed maximum prices on potatoes, milk and bread, but this resulted in shortages, as farmers refused to sell their produce. In 1915, the government decided that pigs were eating too much grain and ordered a 'pig massacre' of 9 million animals. However, this produced a temporary glut of pork, failed to solve the grain shortages and led to a serious lack of fertiliser. Eventually the government took control over the entire food supply. Two meatless days per week were enforced from October 1915. The Imperial Grain Corporation was authorised to buy up the entire grain crop at controlled prices and then ration it out to local governments for distribution. However, the huge bureaucracy failed to overcome the shortages caused by the Allies' blockade and proved incapable of provisioning the cities, even when the daily ration was only 1,000 calories a day in 1917. Suppliers easily evaded the regulations and made tidy profits on the black market.

Desperate labour shortages forced the government to deport to Germany 62,000 workers from occupied countries, but, even so, by 1916 conscription had absorbed 16 per cent of the population, and the labour situation was severe. This was addressed by the 'Hindenburg Programme' and the Auxiliary Labour Law which decreed the closure of the universities and compulsory service in war work or at the Front for all men aged 18–50. Yet profits taxes, reluctantly introduced alongside this, only raised 7.3 billion RM, with the industrial elites embarking upon 'an orgy of profit-making'.[7] The extent of state intervention in Germany seemed, therefore, to be determined as much by the social class concerned, as by the needs of the nation.

After the initial disasters in the war, the Russian government set up in 1915 a series of 'Special Councils' to administer war supplies. These were granted the authority to requisition food, transportation and storage and could demand the co-operation of all public and private institutions. Such sweeping powers were of course hardly new in a country still under the virtual feudal control of the Tsar and his ministers. In fact, the real innovation that the Special Councils brought was in the co-opting of some local zemstvo and municipal boards, which probably meant that supply was carried out with more regard for the concerns of the localities than had been the case previously. However, the Special Councils often clashed with the Army High Command, who resented their interference and continued to issue requisition orders on a grand scale, and with officials, who feared that the zemstvos would prove too capable and thus act as a focus for opposition. The direction of industry was placed in the hands of the Central War Industries Committee. The impact of these measures was patchy. While some parts of the Russian Empire, especially those close to the Front, were stripped of their resources, some remote rural areas barely noticed the war.

Government action was, characteristically, more concerned with 'social control'. The prohibition of the sale of alcohol, according to some historians, led to a dramatic fall in crime (80 per cent down in Petrograd).[8] However, the consumption of other, illegal brews resulted in increased female and adolescent drunkenness. Prostitution was closely regulated. Brothels were taken under police control and 'street-walking' was harshly punished. Again, however, the police failed to appreciate that for many women, especially the young and those refugees forced into cities by the German advance, prostitution was their only means to prevent destitution, which the government failed to alleviate. Attempts to do so, by restricting prices, simply saw products disappear from shops and become procurable only on the black market. The consequences of the government's failure were evident on the streets of every Russian city – 40,000 homeless children, whose fathers were at war, dead or refugees.

The vast increase in the authority of the Great Powers' governments was a matter of wartime expediency, and the post-war period saw capitalist states largely return to pre-war norms. Only Russia, the country where the wartime government had intervened least effectively, witnessed the introduction of a system of wide-scale collectivism, and there it was due to ideological commitment rather than wartime experience. Elsewhere, however, collectivist experiments were not completely forgotten and some institutional aspects of them remained, such as the Ministry of Health in Britain and collective bargaining in Germany. More importantly, perhaps, the benefits of large-scale state intervention were absorbed by politicians, economists and public servants who would become hugely influential with the collapse of free-trade capitalism and the advent of another world war.

Questions

1. How far did the intervention of the state contribute to the victory of the Allies?
2. Did wartime collectivism lead to an acceptance of state intervention after the war?

SOURCES

1. THE FALL OF THE GOVERNMENTS OF 1914

Source A: Bethmann-Hollweg expresses his view of Hindenburg in a telegram, 1916.

The name Hindenburg is a terror to our enemies; it electrifies our army and our people who have a boundless faith in it. Even if we should lose a battle, which God forbid, our people would accept that if Hindenburg were the leader, just as they would accept any peace covered by his name.

Source B: Prussian War Minister, General Wild von Hohenborn, is dismissed, October 1916.

His Majesty, at the behest of Field Marshal von Hindenburg, finds it necessary to give someone else the position of Prussian War Minister. The desirable collaboration between the War Minister and the Supreme Command is no longer taking place. In giving this position to someone new, His Majesty will follow the advice of the Field Marshal.

Source C: Bethmann-Hollweg agrees to adopt unrestricted submarine warfare, 9 February 1917.

When the military authorities consider submarine warfare essential, I am not in a position to object.

Source D: the Tsarina writes to the Tsar, 25 June 1915.

Deary, I heard that that horrid Rodzianko and others went to Goremykin to beg the Duma to be at once called together – oh, please don't, its not their business, they want to discuss things not concerning them and bring more discontent – they must be kept away – I assure you only harm will arise – they speak too much.

Russia, thank God, is not a constitutional country, tho' those creatures try to play a part and meddle in affairs they dare not. Do not allow them to press upon you – its fright if one gives in and their heads will go up.

Source E: Rodzianko's letter to the Tsar, 12 August 1915.

Our native land is going through a painful crisis. General mistrust surrounds the present government, which has lost power and confidence in itself. All idea of authority has been shattered by its disorderly measures. . . . The nation is impatiently longing for a power which will instil confidence and lead the country in the path of victory. Yet at such a time, You decide to displace the Supreme Commander in Chief, whom the Russian people still trusts absolutely. The people will interpret Your step ... as inspired by the Germans around You.

Source F: the *Observer* newspaper on the formation of the first coalition government.

A purely party Cabinet had shown itself to be incapable of dealing with the questions of Drink and Munitions. It would be the less capable afterwards of dealing with other questions bound to arise in connection with what Mr Asquith has called 'the full mobilisation and organisation of our country for war'.

Source G: Georges Clemenceau, vice-president of the Senate Army Commission, attacks the government, 29 May 1915.

When I thought that the government was guilty only of negligence and 'laisser-aller', I did not despair of the final result. But today has been a revelation to me: there has been treason somewhere, and I will not collaborate with treason.

Questions

1. (i) What is meant by 'unrestricted submarine warfare' (Source C)? (2 marks)
    (ii) Who was 'Rodzianko' (Sources D and E)? (2 marks)
2. Does Source A explain the growing power of the German military, as demonstrated in Sources B and C? (4 marks)
*3. Is the Tsarina's letter (Source D) sufficient explanation for the Tsar's rejection of Rodzianko's appeal (Source E)? (5 marks)
4. How far do Sources F and G reveal the causes of political instability in Britain and France to have been similar? (5 marks)
5. In light of the Sources and your own knowledge, would you agree that the pressure of war showed up the weaknesses of the political systems of all the Great Powers? (7 marks)

Worked answer

*3. *[Although the bulk of information necessary to answer a question like this is in the sources, you will need to use some additional information to fully identify the reasons for the Tsar's decision.]*

The Tsarina's advice to Nicholas did, undoubtedly, colour the Tsar's attitude towards politicians such as the President of the Duma, Rodzianko, and caused him to distrust their advice. Alexandra describes Rodzianko as 'horrid', attempting to convince the Tsar that he wants to 'bring more discontent' and 'must be kept away'. Her advice may be seen to influence the Tsar to reject Rodzianko's appeal, for she concludes that 'if one gives in . . . their heads will go up' and they will demand further concessions.

On the other hand, Rodzianko's appeal itself is somewhat clumsy, and the fact that it was published cannot have endeared the author to Nicholas. Rodzianko's tone is extremely critical and his comment that 'The people will interpret Your step . . . as inspired by the Germans around You' is clearly aimed at the Tsar's wife and will only aggravate the Tsar.

The Tsar's main motivation in rejecting the advice of Rodzianko, however, came from his belief in his quasi-mystical position as ruler of Russia. After its disastrous performance, he believed that his duty lay in restoring the shattered morale of his army by demonstrating his personal commitment to the war effort and uniting the country around himself. Certainly the Tsarina encouraged the Tsar in this illusion as well.

SOURCES

2. THE GROWING POWER OF THE STATE

Source H: from the medical journal *The Lancet*, September 1916.

In June 1915, von Hindenburg issued his now notorious order which aimed at a drastic suppression of venereal disease. Briefly, this order threatened with imprisonment for two months to one year any woman who cohabited with soldiers or civilians in spite of the knowledge that she was suffering from venereal disease. Prostitutes who failed to register as such with the police were also liable to a year's imprisonment followed by banishment from the occupied district.

Source I: from DORA, August 1914.

The competent naval or military authority may by order require all premises licensed for the sale of intoxicating liquors within or in the neighbourhood of any defended harbour to be closed except during such hours as may be specified in the order.

Source J: from the War Cabinet Report for the year 1917.

In the same way 1917 may be described as a year in which state control was extended until it covered not only national activities directly affecting the military effort but every section of industry – production, transport and manufacture.

Source K: Russian law on the Special Council to co-ordinate measures for national defence, 1915.

The Special Council is the highest organ created by the state. No government institution or official can issue orders to the Special Council or demand accounting from it.

For the duration of the war:

1. A Special Council to deliberate and co-ordinate all measures for the defense of the state.
2. A Special Council to deliberate and co-ordinate all measures for supplying fuel for transportation purposes ...
3. A Special Council to deliberate and co-ordinate all measures relating to food.
4. A Special Council relating to the transportation of fuel, food and war material.

Signed: .... President of the State Council

On the original His Majesty has written: So Be It.

Source L: An article in the Labour Party newspaper, the *Daily Citizen*, October 1914.

Thus in the hour of its supreme need does the nation turn to the collectivist experiments urged for so many years by the Labour movement, And the experiments are not found wanting. They are abundantly and brilliantly vindicated .... Is it too much to hope that these experiments will still be remembered when these dark, anxious days are at an end? If it be necessary for the State to guard the poor from exploitation now, will it not be sound policy to continue the experiment during what we hope will be the long years of unbroken peace?

Source M: from the *Bulletin of the Federation of British Industries*, October 1918.

Among the business community there is practical unanimity of agreement that there should be as little interference as possible on the part of the State in the future Governance of Industry.

Questions

1. Explain the following references:
   (i) 'von Hindenburg' (Source H). (2 marks)
   (ii) 'DORA' (Source I). (2 marks)
2. What do sources H and I tell you about the attitude of the authorities towards the working classes in Germany and Britain? (4 marks)

3. Contrast the approaches to state intervention illustrated by Sources J and K. (4 marks)

*4. Account for the differing conclusions reached in Sources L and M. (5 marks)

5. After reading all the Sources and in view of your own knowledge, how accurate is it to describe the war as heralding a 'revolution in state control'? (8 marks)

Worked answer

*4. The *Daily Citizen*, a Labour Party newspaper, praises the government for its intervention at the beginning of the war, claiming that such action has been 'abundantly and brilliantly vindicated'. This is because the Labour movement was committed to substantial state intervention to guarantee working and living conditions for all classes, and therefore by extolling the success of wartime collectivism, forced upon the government by circumstances, they hope to convince people that it is a 'sound policy to continue the experiment during . . . the long years of unbroken peace'.

By contrast, the Federation of British Industries, an organisation of private employers, is trying to influence the government at the end of the war to return the direction of industry to private hands. Much industrial activity had been directed by the government during the war, and, despite most having seen considerable profits from government contracts, the 'business community' was eager to return to pre-war conditions with 'as little interference as possible on the part of the State'. Employers wished to take advantage of the expected post-war boom without restrictions on prices, wage settlements and profits.

6

PROTEST AND PACIFISM

BACKGROUND NARRATIVE

The outbreak of war in 1914 led to the proclamation of 'political truces' across Europe, exemplified by the Burgfriede in Germany and the 'Union Sacrée' in France. Everywhere, public opinion was supportive, spurred on by government propaganda. Consequently, there was at first no overt opposition to the war, although some, notably Sergei Witte in Russia and British Labour politicians Keir Hardie and Ramsay Macdonald, expressed reservations. Before long, however, criticism of the war began to emerge, especially amongst socialists. Doubts were expressed regarding both the justification for and the conduct of the war. Anti-war protests occurred in many European cities. Berlin witnessed a peace demonstration by working-class women as early as 1915. Although in France the first street demonstrations only occurred in 1917, prominent socialists like Romain Raillond, labelled 'defeatists' by the public at large, had begun from the outset to campaign for peace. However, these small-scale efforts never posed a realistic threat to the state. The mass of the population continued to support the war effort and to send their loved ones into battle. Conscientious objection was rare, and objectors were treated with contempt and little sympathy, by both state and society.

The events of 1916 challenged this patriotic consensus everywhere. The horrors of the Somme, Verdun and the Eastern Front brought to the surface simmering discontent amongst disaffected soldiers. On the Home Front, shortages, the growing casualty lists, the demands of the wholesale mobilisation of workers and industry, and the failure to achieve a military breakthrough caused a sudden upsurge of unrest and anti-war agitation.

In Russia, dissatisfaction with the conduct of the war had already driven Duma deputies to form the Progressive Bloc in June 1915 which, in concert with industry and the Union of Zemstvos, forced the government to share responsibility for organising the waging of war with a raft of organisations, including the War Industries Committees and Zemgor. Whilst this was explicitly loyalist, the tsarist political police regarded it as an 'opposition', intensifying their surveillance of liberal groups and the Duma. The Tsar clearly shared their analysis, regarding any discontent as evidence of disloyalty and sedition rather than popular criticism of the performance of his government. More concerted resistance to the regime in Russia emerged during 1916. An attempt to mobilise the national minorities led to an uprising in Uzbekistan, which was bloodily put down by troops diverted from front-line duties. In the big cities, the strike movement, which had temporarily subsided in 1914, revived during 1916. The regime simply refused to address the roots of this dissatisfaction, and consequently the unrest continued to develop, culminating in the February Revolution.

Beyond Russia, the strain was apparent too. France experienced a crisis of morale during 1917. The disastrous Nivelle campaign resulted in mutinies at the Front, involving 40,000 soldiers. Between April and June 1917, 250 separate acts of collective indiscipline were recorded in 68 divisions (two-thirds of the French army). On May Day, 10,000 building workers demonstrated in favour of peace. This coincided with a series of strikes, beginning in Parisian textiles and munitions factories in January, and dramatically accelerating during May and June, until hundreds of thousands of workers across France were on strike, demanding improved wages and conditions. Across France local *préfets* reported an alarming slump in morale. The discontent may have contributed to the fall of the government in October, and the appointment of 'the Tiger', Clemenceau. His appointment, and Nivelle's replacement with Pétain, appeared to rescue the situation. By the end of the year, French morale had recovered.

The German strike movement revived during 1916, and demonstrations on the streets of German cities began to appear, starting with a huge demonstration by 60,000 workers, on May Day 1916. In April 1917, 300,000 Berlin workers went on strike, followed by equally large disturbances in Leipzig, Halle and Magdeburg. In each case, women and younger workers were prominent in the disruption. Possibly these new recruits to the workforce, often denied union membership, were unable to protest in any fashion apart from that of spontaneous strike. The government's failure to address the popular concerns thus expressed may have contributed to the ineffectiveness of their Hindenburg Programme.

In Britain, the public mood remained uncompromisingly supportive, but although the consequences were less dramatic and the problems less tangible, even there, the strain was evident. During 1917, 688 strikes occurred, involving 860,000 workers, mainly protesting at the economic effects of war, inflation and changes in working practices, rather than the war itself. Lloyd George was shrewd enough to meet the worries of workers head on, setting up regional commissions to establish the reasons for discontent and to recommend action to alleviate it. Similarly, the wartime efforts of women and working men were rewarded in March 1917 with the passage of a bill to extend the franchise at the end of the war. Such measures helped to stiffen morale against renewed U-boat warfare during 1917. On the Western Front, the British army, although raddled with despair and war-weariness, never organised a serious collective challenge to the authority of command. Even the so-called 'mutiny' at Etaples base camp was little more than a brawl in which a Scots corporal was shot dead by accident and troops took advantage of the confusion to go looting and drinking in the nearby towns. Anger at the camp was directed against the military police rather than the officers and, after a couple of days, the protesters went back to the war.[1]

During 1917, every wartime government faced a crisis of morale. The extent to which the government took steps to meet the concerns of their people with credible promises of reform and concrete measures, determined their ability to ride out the storm and, perhaps, to win the war.

ANALYSIS (1): TO WHAT EXTENT DID 1914–17 SEE THE EMERGENCE OF AN ORGANISED OPPOSITION TO THE WAR?

Although the appalling cost of the war and the deprivations suffered on the Home Front inevitably undermined everywhere the 'political truces' of 1914, it is remarkable how limited was the extent of organised opposition. Only Russia experienced serious resistance to the government before 1917, and opposition only became widespread in Germany during the last few months of the war. Conversely, France survived a serious crisis of morale during 1917 and Britain appears to have suffered least of all. Historians have sought to explain this by contrasting the political cultures of the Western democracies and the authoritarian states of Eastern and Central Europe. Were democracies, paradoxically, more effective at neutralising discontent and opposition than authoritarian states?

In Germany, some middle-class pacifists had attempted to form a German Peace Society, but, faced with uncompromising state repression, their numbers soon dwindled. Opposition from the socialist working classes, however, was potentially much more dangerous, and the growing social and economic pressures of the war led to a huge anti-war demonstration on May Day 1916. Karl Liebknecht, who had broken ranks with the SPD leadership and voted against the war in 1914, addressed this crowd and was arrested, provoking a nationwide strike in support of the martyred socialist. At first most socialist politicians had sought acceptance as valued partners in the national struggle, but in June 1916, all the socialists voted against the budget, in protest against the government's failure to produce plans for political reform.

In March 1917, the Reichstag parties demanded universal suffrage, parliamentary government and immediate peace, and the SPD established a Reichstag committee to consider constitutional reform. Some radical socialists, led by Hugo Haase went further and demanded an immediate end to the war. These radicals had already been expelled from the SPD for opposing war loans and now they formed their own party, the Independent German Social Democratic Party (USPD). The Kaiser, in his Easter Message, responded by promising reform of the Prussian Landtag, a secret ballot and direct elections after the war, but few believed in its sincerity. Consequently, Erzberger's Peace Resolution, supported by socialists and radicals, passed the Reichstag by 212 votes to 126, leading to the resignation of Bethmann-Hollweg and the final collapse of the Burgfriede. Ludendorff's choice of a replacement, Georg Michaelis, was unable to prevent the Reichstag then calling for the reform of the Prussian suffrage, so he too was dismissed. The next chancellor, Georg von Hertling, a 74-year-old Bavarian aristocrat, promised to base his foreign policy on the Peace Resolution and reform the Prussian franchise, thus restoring the Burgfriede, at least temporarily. But isolated incidents, such as the 'naval mutiny' at Wilhelmshaven in August 1917 when 400 sailors refused to obey orders and went on shore without permission, demonstrated that victory had better be quickly forthcoming.

Parliamentary opposition reflected growing popular discontent. Shortages of essentials like coal and bread, deteriorating working conditions, falling wages, worsening inflation and the intrusive regulatory efforts of the state led ordinary Germans to blame the government for the worsening situation. Following the 'turnip winter', a strike movement gathered momentum, with 562 strikes, involving 668,000 workers, occurring during 1917. In January 1918, 1,000,000 workers across Germany struck, demanding peace and democratic reforms. The imposition of martial law swiftly quelled such protest, but could not secure domestic order for long. The OHL had one last opportunity to win the war in 1918, before the factions gathering to end it became irresistible.

Russia experienced greater problems. In January 1916, Tsar Nicholas finally sacked Prime Minister Goremykin, but his replacement, Stuermer, the Court Master of Ceremonies, was a fawning bureaucrat who knew nothing about the war, provoking an angry response from the Kadet, Miliukov: 'What is this: stupidity or treason?' The chasm between the government and the Duma continued to widen. The Octobrist leader, Gutchkov, began plotting with young officers to overthrow Nicholas. In a vain attempt to remove the main focus of criticism, Prince Yusupov and other right-wing aristocrats murdered Rasputin, but all this achieved was to direct criticism towards the Tsar himself. Even members of the royal family began to contemplate action. Sixteen of Nicholas's relations signed a letter begging him not to punish Rasputin's assassins, and Grand Duke Michael was approached by officers wanting to enlist his support for a coup. Indeed, Krymov noted that 'the spirit of the army is such that news of a coup d'état would be welcomed with joy'.

The workers meanwhile had begun to organise themselves. With union activities suspended due to the war, the workers' delegates on the War Industry Committees sought to defend workers' material interests and to raise political issues among the workforce. The Mensheviks in particular envisaged the Workers' Group as the nucleus of a broad-based labour movement which could achieve political reform. Other, more radical voices demanded revolutionary action to end the war. Meanwhile the social crisis deepened, with shortages, hyperinflation and a refugee crisis in Petrograd and Moscow.

In these circumstances the revival of the strike movement is hardly surprising. In 1916 there were 1,284 strikes, involving 952,000 workers. Troops fired on strikers in Kosruma, and the swollen industrial workforce of Moscow and Petrograd became increasingly susceptible to radical socialist agitation. By October 1916, the situation in the cities had grown desperate, the political police reporting that 'the industrial proletariat of the capital is on the verge of despair and . . . the smallest outbreak . . . will lead to uncontrollable riots'. Revolution was in the air.

Invaded France had no difficulties in mobilising popular support for the war effort. Throughout the conflict, the French people exhibited a grim determination to fight 'jusqu'au bout'[2] to expel the invader. Organised opposition was slow in emerging and ineffective when it did appear. The opposition Socialist Party accepted the 'Union Sacrée' and curtailed its activities. However, once the immediate danger of France being overrun by German forces in September had been averted, a few radicals began to express pacifist views. *Le Midi Socialiste* attacked the 'sadness, suffering, ruin and death', and from exile the socialist Romain Rolland criticised the war.[3] In May 1915, the Haute Vienne Socialist Federation demanded 'an end to the war . . . in the interests of socialism, of the working class and of our country',[4] but gained little public sympathy for its stance. The first anti-war demonstration occurred only in January 1917, when 400 women protested in St Junien.

There was criticism of the conduct of the war, however. In 1915 the Paris Prefect of Police noted the growing discontent regarding prices, rents, wages and conditions of work.[5] It was believed, and bitterly resented, that the wealthy were obtaining releases from front-line duty, leaving the poor to shoulder the burden of the fighting. Even so, for much of the war, France remained calm.

Opposition gathered force suddenly and spectacularly during May 1917, when the failure of Nivelle's offensive, rapid price increases and the first stirrings of front-line mutiny sparked off strikes across France. The mutineers had no organisation, however, nor any clearly defined political programme. Although the scale of the disruption alarmed the whole nation, it was very rarely violent, mostly involving a refusal to return to the front line and demands for more leave and an end to the suicidal Nivelle offensive. The strikes which followed involved hundreds of thousands of workers across France. Government censors reported an increasingly despondent and rebellious mood among the population, citing complaints that 'Life in Paris is terrible. . . . We simply have to put an end to this war. . . . Food is far too expensive.'[6] Ordinary people bitterly criticised government corruption and the press seized upon scandals involving ministers. Yet workers at strike meetings largely ignored efforts by prominent pacifists like Merrheim to recruit their support for an end to the war. Protests primarily targeted specific economic grievances, and the determined mood of 'jusqu'au boutisme' remained.

The spring and summer of 1917 were a crossroads for French public morale. Why did France hold out? The appointment of Pétain, popular with the troops, as military commander, ended the soldiers' protests. America's declaration of war and the fall of the Tsar led people to anticipate a final marshalling of forces to defeat the Germans. Finally, the appointment of Clemenceau clearly galvanised public morale for one last effort. Overall it appears that pacifist and anti-war opinion never took hold of the vast majority of the French public, although popular morale dipped alarmingly during 'l'année troublée' of 1917.

In Britain, the absence of anti-war sentiment is striking. Despite the passage of the Defence of the Realm Act in August 1914, by which the government obtained extensive powers to control public opinion and opposition, the state rarely felt the need to deploy its powers against the ranks of the dissenters and pacifists.

This was because there were very few of them. On the political left, groups like the Herald League and the Workers' Socialist Foundation campaigned against the war from the outset, but gained very little public support, garnering dozens rather than hundreds of members.[7] The Union of Democratic Control (UDC), founded by Charles Trevalyan on 5 August 1914, was larger, but it campaigned for a peaceful *post-war* world rather than an immediate end to the war. The 'No Conscription Fellowship', formed by Clifford Allen in response to the Military Service Act in 1915, had only a limited impact. Primarily supported by religious dissenters (especially Quakers), socialists and radical feminists, and numbering amongst its energetic and dedicated supporters such luminaries as Bertrand Russell, Fenner Brockway and Sylvia Pankhurst, it provided moral and legal assistance to men who refused to serve. However, in the event, only 16,100 men 'objected'. Furthermore, objectors received very little support or sympathy from the public as a whole. Disappointingly for these (mostly) socialist campaigners, the working classes rejected utterly conscientious objection, pacifism and even moderation in British war aims. The Labour Party itself remained deeply divided over demands for peace, with principle jostling with the achievement of power in Lloyd George's Cabinet. The press lambasted and ridiculed campaigners, and their meetings were disrupted. Indeed, the state seems judiciously to have left the task of discrediting and disrupting the activities of 'pacifists' to the people themselves.

There was, however, growing industrial unrest as the war continued. Workers were aggrieved over 'shaking-out', rising prices for coal and food, stagnant wages, the increasing 'dilution' of skilled work through the introduction of unskilled (often female) labour and new, mechanised processes, the high cost of housing and rents, and the perceived failure of the government to honour its promises regarding reserved occupations. Despite Lloyd George's efforts to recruit the support of the union movement, huge strikes during 1915 immobilised the Welsh mining areas and Clydeside. A further wave of strikes affected Britain during 1917, but the government's policy of meeting strikers' demands, establishing rent controls and granting war bonuses and concessions to workers, minimised the disruption. It is noticeable, however, that the German offensive of March 1918 was marked by a lull in industrial action, suggesting that British workers were prepared to put the need to win the war before their own demands.

The only notable armed opposition came from Ireland, where a collection of Republican extremists, who had rejected Redmond's call to serve in the army, decided that 'England's difficulty is Ireland's opportunity' and contacted the German authorities to supply guns for an uprising. The Easter Rising of 1916 may have marked the first declaration of an Irish Republic, but to most Dubliners and to the British army, who crushed it in a week with the loss of 116 men, such rebels were traitors, who discredited the Irish cause by their actions. It was the British response to the rising that shifted sympathy towards the republicans.

It is evident that Britain experienced less discontent than elsewhere during 1915–17. Why was this? Britain's smaller commitment of manpower, and therefore fewer casualties, than France, Germany or Russia may partially explain the relative quiet on the Home Front. Certainly the economic strain was less keenly felt in Britain and France, as imports were maintained, serious bread shortages never really affected the public, and rationing was only introduced during the final year of the war. It appears that, by paying greater attention to the subsistence needs of their people on the Home Front, Britain and France prevented the emergence of significant anti-war opposition. Secondly, the British army, at least, was made up of what J.M. Winter has described as 'the most highly disciplined industrial labour force in the world'[8] and it seemed quite prepared to continue to obey orders. Collective behaviour like that at Etaples, or individual behaviour like that of Lieutenant Siegfried Sassoon, who published a condemnation of the war, was significant only because of its rarity. Why the vast majority of soldiers of all armies kept fighting without complaint remains ultimately a matter for conjecture. Were they convinced by the tightly controlled propaganda of their state? Did they genuinely believe that they were fighting for their homes and their families? Or were they simply so used to obeying the orders of those they had been indoctrinated from birth to regard as their superiors?

Questions

1. Why did 1916 and 1917 witness an upsurge in popular discontent on the Home Fronts of each of the Great Powers?
2. To what extent and why were Britain and France more successful in handling popular unrest than Germany and Russia?

ANALYSIS (2): HOW DID THE GOVERNMENTS OF EUROPE RESPOND TO PACIFISM AND OPPOSITION TO THE WAR?

'Total War' invariably results in the expansion of the state's authority and diminished personal freedoms. The necessity of ensuring and, if necessary, enforcing national unity leads inexorably to the growth of state coercive power and its deployment against dissent and opposition. Regrettably, principled resistance to the very concept of war can, under such circumstances, come to be regarded as disloyalty. Yet one of the striking contrasts between the 'democracies' in Western Europe, and the more authoritarian states of Central and Eastern Europe was the response of the state to opposition and pacifism.

The experience of war turned into pacifists many who had not been so in 1913, although we should also note that many 'pacifists' of 1913 – for example, the German SPD and the Anglican Church – became supporters of the war too. Consequently, pacifism became a more and more urgent issue as the war progressed. Conscientious objection was perhaps more of an issue in Britain than in invaded France or authoritarian Germany and Russia. Even so, governments in every European state almost invariably responded to objection in uncompromising fashion.

In Britain, the Defence of the Realm Act (DORA), passed in the first days of the war, considerably restricted personal liberty, with the government assuming the power to court martial anyone 'jeopardising the success of the operations of His Majesty's forces or assisting the enemy'.[9] This was later extended to cover 'spreading disaffection'. Remarkably, however, the state used its extensive powers sparingly. Rather than deploy DORA against the strikers in South Wales and Clydeside in 1915, Lloyd George chose instead to pacify them with concessions, war bonuses and reforms. 'Joint Industrial Councils' were initiated to draw the unions into partnership with the government, and Lloyd George continued this approach when he became Prime Minister, appointing Henderson to his inner 'war cabinet' and two other Labour MPs as ministers of state. For the most part the state relied on the patriotic enthusiasm of the people, and of the press in particular, to squash expressions of dissent and limit the effectiveness of 'anti-war' campaigns.

The same approach was taken towards 'conchies' with, it may be argued, considerable success. The 'No Conscription Fellowship' never posed the government a realistic challenge regarding the morality of conscription or on the wider issue of the war itself. Only 16,100 men 'objected', and these, when brought before the conscientious objection tribunals, often received surprisingly lenient treatment. Four-fifths received some form of exemption, and the remainder by and large were allocated non-combatant duties. Even so, in the end many served prison sentences, and 71 died in prison, some after torture, such as mock firing squads, force-feeding and being suspended off the ground with a 20 lb. weight tied to their feet for 28 hours,[10] which reflected ill on Britain's claim to be defending civilisation against 'German barbarism'.

In general, however, the government's handling of opposition and conscientious objection was distinguished by its skill and lightness of touch. Lloyd George seems to have appreciated that the population as a whole had little sympathy with 'shirkers', and he showed an acute awareness of the value of meeting the welfare needs of the working people during the conflict. By ensuring that labour was won over, through the approval of arbitration tribunals, rent controls, price fixing and eventually rationing, the government ensured that the public at large, for all their weariness, remained supportive of the war and therefore unreceptive to the arguments of the peace lobby. Given this, the government felt able (largely) to ignore these voices, although prominent campaigners, like the UDC's Morel, did serve jail sentences. In Ireland, however, a different approach was taken and 15 of the leaders of the Easter Rising were executed by firing squad. This caused such a storm of protest that the shootings were stopped and Lloyd George, as War Minister, was dispatched to try to calm the country. As Prime Minister, he continued to try to mollify the Irish, until manpower shortages on the Western Front drove him to threaten to extend conscription to Ireland (it had been exempted in 1916, for fear of provoking riots). The reaction of the nationalist community was so strong that Lloyd George was forced to withdraw the threat, but not before Sinn Fein had become the most influential political movement in the south. Lloyd George's attempts to untangle the Irish problem would see him continuing to veer from violent coercion to friendly co-operation after the war.

Elsewhere in Europe there was precious little evidence of conscientious objection on a large scale, although every continental state experienced opposition to the war. In France, aside from the vocal opposition of socialists such as Romain Raillond, the fact of German invasion and occupation served to mobilise even the syndicalist opponents of war. It was left to a handful of radicals like Merrheim and Caillaux to resist on behalf of those few Frenchmen who rejected 'jusqu'au boutisme'. The state's response was uncompromising. After overcoming the mutinies and strikes of 1917, the government turned on radical voices and newspapers. *Le Bonnet Rouge*, a left-wing paper, was closed down, and its editor, Duval, arrested and tried for treason, along with 1,700 others. Caillaux's 'defeatism' resulted in his arrest and trial in 1918 for treason, to public acclaim. Most famously of all, Malvy, Minister of the Interior between 1914 and 1917, received a sentence of banishment for his (lesser) 'crimes'.[11] The pacifist case was denied the oxygen of publicity through the exercise of censorship, under the auspices of the Interior Ministry. The press, for the most part, needed no encouragement to vilify and attack the 'defeatist' case. The people as a whole showed similar disregard for the pacifist argument. One mother, whose son had deserted because 'we are all fed up with killing', handed him over to the authorities, because 'I have already lost one son in the war. I want him to finish his duty until this whole terrible business is over.'[12] Such attitudes pervaded French society and consequently the state had little need for coercive measures against pacifists. However, as we have seen, popular discontent with the conduct of the war did emerge, especially during 1917. Then, in the face of strikes, anti-war demonstrations and, more damagingly, front-line mutinies, the French state adopted a similar approach to that evident across the channel. Workers' demands for better conditions, price controls and wage increases were treated with sympathy by Albert Thomas at the Ministry of Armaments, although Clemenceau, once installed as Prime Minister in 1917, showed less understanding. Pétain arrested and punished mutineers, but out of 3,427 soldiers found guilty of mutiny, only 49 were actually executed. Many of the mutineers' demands were met by Pétain, who immediately announced a war of defence in which the priority would be to minimise further loss of French life.

Because the 'democracies' depended upon mass participation and compliance for their legitimacy, they relied to a greater extent upon 'self-mobilisation', and generally shied away from repression when seeking to enforce uniformity and support for the national effort. Instead, persuasion was relied upon, and this was often left to semi-official and private agencies. Even amidst the crisis of 1917, this remained true. Faced with working-class economic protests and discontent brought about by deteriorating conditions, the state in Britain and France granted concessions, whilst reserving their coercive efforts for explicitly pacifist protest. Even so, both governments quickly recognised that, with a relatively unregimented press, any public pursuit of 'defeatists' provided them with a platform to express their views. Some of those prosecuted received significant public sympathy – for example, Helene Brion in France. Both the British and French governments increasingly focused their fire upon less sympathetic targets, so as to create the morale-boosting impression of a tough line on 'defeatists' and 'traitors', whilst allowing the continued expression of dissenting opinion, as the survival of papers such as *Labour Leader* and *La Vague* indicates. The govern-ment relied upon its own propaganda efforts and those of private patriotic associations like the NWAC and UGAPE, both of which existed half within and half outside the government, to dilute the impact of the anti-war opposition. Meanwhile, in Germany, the OHL sponsored the formation of the radical right-wing group, the Fatherland Party, which sought to revive unquestioning public support for the regime's war effort. But the absence of any genuine popular acceptance of the military regime dampened the effects of this effort.

In Germany, a few principled intellectual or religious opponents of war, notably George Grosz, resisted conscription and received jail sentences for their pains. However, on the whole, German soldiers obeyed the call to arms, although their bitter dissatisfaction with the conduct of the war became increasingly evident. German soldiers' letters and diaries exhibit little jingoism after 1914, and a growing readiness to absorb the propaganda of the radical Left at home is evident.[13]

Criticism of the war on the Home Front became more widespread after 1916 and, despite the existence of censorship, enforced through the military governors of each region, hostile opinion was difficult to muzzle. Germany possessed more newspapers than any other state, and these increasingly questioned the conduct of the war. The *Berliner Tagblatt* attacked the seizure of industrial assets from occupied terri-tories; other newspapers reported openly the increasingly commonplace street demonstrations; and even the moderate *Frankfurter Zeitung* called for a negotiated and honourable peace.[14] The authorities did attempt to muzzle the most visible manifestations of opposition by arresting prominent critics. Liebknecht and other radical socialists, especially those associated with the newsletter *Spartacus*, spent much of the war in jail. During the strikes of January 1918, a declaration of martial law in Berlin restored order, but it could not revive the 'spirit of 1914' or coax renewed commitment to the war effort from the workforce. Workers' Councils were formed, on the Russian model, and the only weapon the authorities possessed against them was forcible conscription of the ringleaders to front-line duties, which had little effect on the mutinous mood of the workers. Indeed, it may have accelerated the spread of revolutionary ideas among the troops themselves.

In Russia, the authoritarian regime of Nicholas II was unable to appreciate what Lloyd George and Thomas saw so clearly. From the outset of the conflict, the government instructed its department of political police, Fontanka, to monitor opposition. There was little understanding of the potential value of enlisting the support of former critics in a national crusade. Pre-war assumptions of the relationship between the regime and the 'other Russia' remained, preventing ministers and police chiefs alike from interpreting accurately the events which followed.

The Okhrana (tsarist secret police) was unable even to effectively gather intelligence and inform the government. Agents were conscripted into the army, and its personnel was cut back at precisely the moment when its duties were being expanded. Furthermore, the 'ministerial leapfrog' which characterised central government politics during the war prevented the development of a coherent policy or a sustained analysis of what intelligence was gathered. There were six Ministers of the Interior during 1915–17, and five Heads of the political police. Cronyism and nepotism prevailed, and many of those heading the fight against subversion were incompetent or corrupt. Fontanka was, in the words of Klimovich, 'completely without a rudder, without a sail, not knowing what to do'.

Consequently, the police fell back on pre-war tactics and assumptions, regarding the Duma and the Progressive Bloc as suspect, Zemgor as a challenge to the government's authority and the Central War Industries Committee as a hotbed of revolutionaries agitating for a constitution. Even so, as the crisis developed during 1916, the penny began to drop amongst some officials. Martynov, Head of the Moscow Special Division, concluded in October that 'it is difficult to name a class of society which will stand solidly with the government'.[15] However, the Interior Ministry refused to hear such unpalatable news, and demanded that the 'ringleaders' be rounded up, so as to forestall revolution. In vain, police officials argued that the malaise ran a lot deeper than a few activists, that the movement was popular and spontaneous. As late as February, Vasiliev, the incompetent director of Fontanka, assured the Tsaritsa that 'Revolution as such was quite impossible.'[16] When the uprising eventually came, the Head of the Petrograd bureau was baffled, because it was 'without any party preparation and without preliminary . . . plans'.[17] The tsarist regime failed to deal effectively with dissent during the war because they completely misunderstood the nature, extent and purpose of the opposition expressed.

Whilst pacifist opinion and general anti-war dissent during the First World War met with a subtle and compromising response from the 'democracies' of Western Europe, the German state showed little understanding of the need to placate its discontented populace, and failed to address the causes of discontent. Instead, they placed all their hopes in a victory which would paper over the divisions in German society. Meanwhile, in Russia, all dissent was met with ineffective repression. It is evident that the policy of meeting opposition halfway was significantly more successful than the authoritarian approach. Certainly the police-state methods employed in Russia were singularly ineffective, contributing to the revolution rather than averting it.

Questions

1. Why was there so little support for pacifist opposition to the First World War?
2. Compare and contrast the Great Powers' response to the expression of anti-war opinion on the Home Front.

SOURCES

1. THE SPREAD OF WAR-WEARINESS

Source A: from a report of the Portuguese Ambassador in Berlin, 1916.

The German people are feeling the pinch of the war . . . but are far too disciplined to do more than grumble, for a long time to come. The result of the war is not in doubt, but the allies must be prepared for a protracted and sullen resistance on the part of Germany, and ought not to underestimate the difficulty of wearing down the spirit of a people which, after all, is profoundly patriotic and schooled to accept with fatalistic resignation the decisions of its government . . . Nothing justifies the supposition that the German masses are likely to revolt against the authorities for many a long day.

Source B: statistics of strikes in Germany.

Year	Strikes
1912	2,500
1913	2,100
1914	?
1915	137
1916	240
1917	561
1918	531

Source C: from a Prefect's report of anti-war demonstrations in Paris, May Day 1917.

As they left the hall, cries of 'Long live peace! Down with the war! Down with the republic!' mingled with the chanting of the 'Internationale' and of 'Revolution', could be heard on all sides.

In the passage that leads to the rue Grange-aux-Belles, one-legged Meric, surrounded by members of the Trade Union Youth Movement and by Russians, invited passers-by to a demonstration on the place de la Republique and on the grand boulevards.

At the end of the passage a crowd intoned revolutionary songs and moved towards the Boulevard Magenta in great excitement. Once again there were cries of 'Down with the war! Long live peace!' and even 'Long live Germany!'

Source D: a historian examines the front-line mutinies in France, 1917.

250 cases of collective insubordination among combat troops, although never while in the line of fire; these acts of insubordination affected, on various dates, units in half the infantry divisions, the total of those affected probably reaching 40,000, although each act involved small groups of men only, often less than 100. In only 1 case did the movement reflect political ends: mutineers in 1 infantry division called for a march on Paris. A study of this crisis has revealed that its main cause was the failure of the major offensive of 16 April; the infantrymen had no wish to be called on to resume offensive operations that had been so badly handled by the High Command, although they did declare that they were ready to resist any German attack. When the crisis was over, the morale of the army recovered quickly.

Source E: a British Socialist and member of the Clyde Workers Committee, remembers.

War was declared, and the male portion of our army of strikers vanished within 24 hours to line up at the nearest recruiting offices to fight for the country which was only giving them the meanest level of existence . . . .

The life of a member of the ILP was one of stress and struggle while the war lasted. We were 'white-livered curs', 'bloody pro-Germans', friends of the Kaiser, traitors to our country. A large proportion of our members, particularly elected persons, left us or withdrew from all activities . . . .

One weekend (in 1916) I went to London to attend a meeting of the No Conscription Fellowship. When I returned to Glasgow it was to learn that the active men in the Clyde Workers Committee had been seized from their homes during the previous night and had been carted away somewhere out of Glasgow, no one knew where. . . . A few days afterwards I also was arrested in the middle of the night, and after a period of some weeks in jail was tried and sentenced to twelve months' imprisonment for a breach of the Defence of the Realm Act . . . .

Source F: Siegfried Sassoon's statement of protest against the war, 1917.

I am making this statement as an act of wilful defiance of military authority, because I believe that the War is being deliberately prolonged by those who have the power to end it. I am a soldier, convinced that I am acting on behalf of soldiers. I believe that this War, upon which I entered as a war of defence and liberation, has now become a war of aggression and conquest. I believe that the purposes for which I and my fellow-soldiers entered upon this War should have been so clearly stated as to have made it impossible for them to be changed without our knowledge, and that, had this been done, the objects which actuated us would now be attainable by negotiation.

I have seen and endured the sufferings of the troops, and I can no longer be a party to prolonging those sufferings for ends which I believe to be evil and unjust.

Questions

*1. Explain the references above to:
    (i) 'the failure of the major offensive of 16 April' (Source D). (2 marks)
    (ii) 'the ILP' (Source E). (2 marks)
2. To what extent does Source B support the judgement of the Portuguese ambassador in Source A? (4 marks)
3. How useful might Source E be to a historian examining the extent of dissent in Britain during the war? (5 marks)
4. Comment on the effectiveness of the tone and content of Source F. (5 marks)
5. Using all the extracts above, and your own knowledge, critically assess the view that every European state witnessed a crisis of morale during 1916–17. (7 marks)

Worked answer

*1. (i) This refers to the Nivelle Offensive launched during April 1916 in the Chemin des Dames area, which resulted in huge casualties and a rash of mutinies.

*1. (ii) This refers to the Independent Labour Party, a proportion of which became active in the pacifist and strike movements during the war.

SOURCES

2. GROWING OPPOSITION IN RUSSIA

Source G: Petrograd Political Police Report on the situation in Russia, October 1916.

The industrial proletariat is on the verge of despair, and ... the smallest outbreak, due to any pretext, will lead to uncontrollable riots, with thousands and tens of thousands of victims. Indeed the stage for such outbreaks is more than set: the economic position of the masses ... is distressing .... The impossibility of obtaining, even for cash, many foodstuffs and articles of prime necessity, the waste of time involved in spending hours waiting in line in front of stores, the increasing morbidity due to inadequate diet and insanitary lodgings (cold and dampness as a result of lack of coal and firewood) etc., all these conditions have created such a situation that the mass of industrial workers are quite ready to let themselves go to the wildest excesses of a hunger riot ....

In addition to economic hardships the 'legal disabilities' of the working class have of late become 'intolerable and unbearable'.

Source H: statistics of strikes in Russia.

Year	Strikes	Strikers
1905	13,995	2,863,000
1913	2,404	887,000
1914 (total)	3,535	1,337,000
1914 (Aug–Dec)	68	35,000
1915	928	540,000
1916	1,234	952,000
1917 (Jan–Feb)	1,330	676,000

Source I: the Council Of Ministers discuss the problem of recruiting, August 1915.

Scherbatov: Recruiting is going from bad to worse. The police is unable to handle the slackers. They hide in the forest and in the grain fields. If it should become known that the recruits of the second class are called out without the approval of the Duma I fear that, under the present conditions, we would not get a single man.

Source J: Trotsky on the dissolution of the army.

The Russian army lost in the war more men than any army which ever participated in a national war – approximately two and a half million killed .... In the first months the soldiers fell under shell fire unthinkingly . . . but from day to day they gathered experience – bitter experience of the lower ranks who are ignorantly commanded. They measured the confusion of the generals by the number of purposeless manoeuvres on sole-less shoes, the number of dinners not eaten . . . .

The swiftest of all to disintegrate was the peasant infantry. As a general rule, the artillery, with its high percentage of industrial workers, is distinguished by an incomparably greater hospitality to revolutionary ideas. This was clearly evident in 1905. If in 1917, on the contrary, the artillery showed more conservatism than the infantry, the cause lies in the fact that through the infantry divisions, as through a sieve, there passed ever new and less and less trained human masses. The artillery, moreover, suffering infinitely fewer losses, retained its original cadres . . . . But in the long run the artillery yielded too. During the retreat from Galicia a secret order was issued by the commander-in-chief; 'flog the soldiers for desertion and other crimes'. The soldier Pereiko relates, 'they began to flog soldiers for the most trivial offences; for example, for a few hours' absence without leave. And sometimes they flogged them in order to rouse their fighting spirit.' As early as September 17, 1915, Kuropatkin wrote, citing Gutchkov, 'the lower orders began the war with enthusiasm; but now they are weary, and with the continual retreats have lost faith in a victory'.

Source K: Miliukov attacks the Tsar's government, November 1916.

We now see and know that we can no more legislate with this government than we can lead Russia to victory with it. . . . We say to this government, as the Declaration of the Bloc stated, 'We will fight you; we will fight by all legal means until you go . . .' When the Duma . . . declares again and again that the home front must be organised for a successful war and the government . . . consciously chooses chaos and disorganisation – is this stupidity or treason?

Questions

1. Briefly explain the significance of the following individuals:
   (i) 'Gutchkov' (Source I). (2 marks)
   (ii) 'Miliukov' (Source K). (2 marks)
2. In light of Sources G and H, what problems would the Russian government have in sustaining the war effort? (4 marks)
3. What do Sources I and J tell us about the performance of the Russian army during the war? (4 marks)
4. Critically evaluate the reliability and usefulness of Source J to a historian studying the state of the Russian army during the war. (5 marks)

*5. 'It is difficult to name a class of society which would stand solidly with the government.' To what extent do the Sources, and your own knowledge, support Martynov's judgement of the situation by the end of 1916 in Russia? (8 marks)

Worked answer

*5. *[This question will require more time and more careful development than the other sections, and you should allocate 15 minutes to answer it. It is important that you focus on the question and that your answer draws upon all the relevant documents, which should be referred to by letter. It is most effective to integrate references to the sources into a coherent answer to the question, as has been done below, rather than work through the documents one by one and then tag your own knowledge on the end. The latter approach is clumsy and inelegant.]*

Martynov argues that the Tsar's government stood isolated by the end of 1916, and his view is supported by the sources above. Early in the war, the peasants and workers fighting at the Front began to lose faith in their government, as Sources I and J indicate. The appalling losses (Trotsky gives a figure of 2,500,000, although other historians have set the figure at 1,800,000 dead and 3 million prisoners or 'missing') and the dreadful shortages of essentials like boots and bayonets forced the rank and file to conclude that their Tsar either did not care for them or was incapable of leading them effectively. Either way, as Source I suggests, by the middle of 1915, peasants were evading the draft and, by the end of 1916, even the generals could see that the army 'would welcome news of a coup' (General Krymov). This dissatisfaction was evident on the Home Front too, where the workers, desperate for regular supplies of bread, overworked and cold, due to severe coal shortages, expressed their discontent through riots and strikes, which often took political form, demanding an end to the war and a responsible government, elected by the people. The strike movement, which had virtually vanished during the early days of the war, revived with a vengeance in 1916 and reached a crescendo in January 1917 (Sources G and H).

Their political representatives in the Duma had reached the same state of exasperation with the Tsar's ineffectual government and stubborn resistance to reform. The Duma had taken the step in June 1915 of forming a united front, the 'Progressive Bloc', to pressurise the regime into granting reforms. At first the object of this regrouping of political parties was to force the Tsar to accept the assistance of the political classes in the management of the war, so as to achieve victory. The members of the bloc did not see themselves as rebels, rather that they were saving tsarism from defeat and rebellion. However, the Tsar's response to their efforts was half-hearted. His political police were instructed to monitor the 'revolutionary centre' in the Duma, and the Council of Ministers rejected much of the advice and assistance offered over the next 18 months, such that, by November 1916, the gulf between the Duma and the Tsar was as great as ever. Miliukov's forceful and courageous attack on the Tsar's government (not, we should remember, on the Tsar himself) in Source K indicates the extent to which the two bodies had parted company, and further supports Martynov's judgement.

By February 1917, even members of the royal family had lost faith in the Tsar's regime, and were listening sympathetically to senior military figures demanding a coup against the government. When the revolution began, Martynov's prediction was borne out – not a single group in Russian society rallied to defend the Tsar.

7

THE FALL OF THE RUSSIAN AND GERMAN GOVERNMENTS

BACKGROUND NARRATIVE

In 1917 Russia was plunged into a deep political crisis. Whilst the Tsar and Tsarina mourned Rasputin, a creeping paralysis afflicted the government. Generals, politicians and even members of the imperial family, desperate to avert defeat and revolution, began to consider a coup. Discontented urban workers staged a series of increasingly political strikes, beginning with a demonstration marking the anniversary of Bloody Sunday on 9 January. Further strikes occurred in February, led by the politically active Putilov steelworkers. Ominously, their banners proclaimed 'Down with the Tsar' and 'Down with the War'. On 23 February (International Women's Day), amidst rumours of further cuts in bread rations, Petrograd's women joined the protest. By 25 February a general strike was in progress. The commander of the Petrograd garrison, Khabarov, reported that his troops were deserting or refusing to leave their barracks and the police and the militia were joining in demonstrations.

On 27 February the Menshevik-dominated Petrograd Soviet reconvened in the Tauride Palace, calling for a Constituent Assembly elected by universal suffrage. Elsewhere in the same building, the leading Duma politicians, including Rodzianko, Miliukov, Shulgin and Kerensky, formed a 'Provisional Committee of the Duma' 'for the restoration of order'. A government-in-waiting now existed. Nicholas decided to return to Petrograd, hoping to rally the loyalist forces that he believed existed. However, his train was stopped on 1 March at Pskov, where a delegation of generals and Duma representatives, led by Shulgin, demanded his abdication. Nicholas abdicated on 2 March, but his chosen successor, his brother Grand Duke Michael, refused the crown. Thus Romanov rule ended, and the Provisional Committee found itself in charge of Russia.

The Provisional Government was hobbled from the start by its own questionable legitimacy, and the confusing 'Dual Authority' it shared with the Petrograd Soviet. Although the two bodies co-operated to restore order and introduce reforms, deep-seated differences existed from the outset regarding the continuation of the war. The Soviet's 'Order Number 1' undermined military discipline and made them the effective masters of the army, and when the new Foreign Minister, Miliukov, tried to reassure Russia's allies that she remained committed to the war, the 'Miliukov Note' sparked street demonstrations.

Nonetheless, during the next six months, the Provisional Government grappled vainly with the manifold problems bequeathed them – industrial unrest, rampant inflation, military defeat and growing rural discontent. It proved impossible, however, to address these issues in wartime, and the new government had no intention of ending Russian involvement in the war, believing that victory was possible now that they had assumed responsibility for the war effort. Consequently, 1917 witnessed a valiant effort to remobilise the weary Russian people for the war. In June, the Socialist War Minister, Kerensky, launched a huge offensive which, after initial gains, failed disastrously, resulting in street demonstrations – the July Days. These evolved into an abortive coup by left-wing activists, for which the Bolsheviks were (probably inaccurately) blamed. However, the government failed to capitalise on its success and when in August elements on the Right launched their own coup, the Kornilov Revolt, Kerensky, by then the leader of the fledgling republic, fell back upon the Left to 'save the revolution', and released and armed the Bolsheviks arrested in July.

By September, the government's authority had evaporated. The Bolsheviks, victorious in both the Moscow and Petrograd city council elections, controlled the Soviet; the strike movement had revived; peasants around the country were forcibly repartitioning the land; and the army had collapsed. When the Bolsheviks launched their successful coup in Petrograd in October, few defended the government. 'Red October', the second Russian revolution of 1917, was relatively bloodless.

The final crisis of the German regime began in July 1918, with the collapse of the Ludendorff Offensive. On 8 August, the 'Black Day of the German Army', the German line finally broke under the Allied counter-attack, and the army began to retreat. As Germany's allies surrendered, Ludendorff counselled the government in September that Germany had lost the war and faced invasion from abroad and revolution at home. The chancellor accordingly contacted United States President Wilson, requesting an immediate peace based on his '14 Points'.

Shortly afterwards, the OHL gathered at Hindenburg's headquarters at Spa. Ludendorff argued that democratic reforms should immediately be introduced (a 'revolution from above'), so as to forestall a Communist revolution, *pace* Russia. He contended furthermore that the Allies would inflict a less painful peace upon a fellow democracy, leaving the OHL to retake control later.

The Kaiser concurred, duly appointing his liberal cousin, Prince Max of Baden, to head a new, reformist government, which for the first time included members of the Majority SPD (MSPD). Ministers were to be responsible to the Reichstag; the army was placed under civilian control; and the Prussian Landtag was to be reformed. However, when peace negotiations opened on 4 October, Allied demands made it clear that the time for negotiation was already past. As Prince Max observed, 'I believed that I had been summoned at five minutes to twelve and find that it is already five minutes past.' Angrily (shrewdly?), Ludendorff resigned on 26 October, to be replaced by General Groener, a 'moderate' who had the confidence of the labour leaders.

Meanwhile, with the realisation that the war was lost, mass opinion in Germany radicalised spectacularly. Fearing a workers' revolution, industrialists forged deals with the more moderate unions. Workers' councils were formed, demanding an end to the war and the Kaiser's abdication. The increasingly volatile situation finally erupted at Kiel, when the admirals of the High Seas Fleet ordered a final suicide attack on the Royal Navy on 28 October. The sailors, underfed and bitter at years of inaction, mutinied. In Bavaria, fear of an Allied invasion after Austria-Hungary's surrender led Kurt Eisner, a radical member of

USPD, to seize control of the Bavarian government on 7 November, declaring an independent Bavarian Republic. As the unrest spread, the government quickly realised that only the Kaiser's abdication could avert revolution.

Amidst growing anarchy, Groener informed the Kaiser on 9 November: 'The army will retire rapidly and orderly to the homeland under the command of its leaders and commanding generals, but not under the command of Your Majesty, whom it no longer supports.' Wilhelm fled to Holland that night. Meanwhile, Max had resigned, leaving the country without a government, and the people thronged the Berlin streets, where radical socialists like Liebknecht announced (to unimpressed crowds) the formation of a revolutionary socialist state. Max's nominee as chancellor, Friedrich Ebert, leader of the MSPD, dithered, preferring a constitutional monarchy. However, events could not wait. On 10 November, Ebert's colleague Philip Schiedemann declared, from the balcony of the Reichstag, 'Long live the Great German Republic!' Although this forestalled the declaration of a Communist republic, the situation was now very confused, as the new government had no legitimate constitutional right to rule. Amidst renewed street violence, Groener offered Ebert the army's assistance in crushing the Communists and the break-away Bavarian Republic. Ebert, with one eye on the situation in Russia and fearing a Bolshevik coup by the Spartacists, agreed, promising not to reform the army. This deal ensured the restoration of order, but it also guaranteed the survival of the military caste. Thus the 'German Revolution' was crippled at birth.

ANALYSIS (1): WHY DID THE FIRST WORLD WAR RESULT IN THE FALL OF THE REGIME IN RUSSIA?

Historians largely agree that the war was the crucial factor in the fall of tsarism, but its precise role is the subject of continued debate, as are the reasons for the success of the Bolsheviks in October. Soviet and Marxist historians, the so-called 'Pessimists', stress the historical logic of events, arguing that antiquated tsarism was heading inexorably for revolution in 1914, but that the war brought to the fore the inadequacies of the regime and assisted the historical process. Lyaschenko observed that 'The war was, in Lenin's expression, "A mighty accelerator of the process of revolutionisation".'[1] 'Pessimists' characterise the war as a catalyst for the inevitable march of History, and greater stress is laid upon the repressive character of tsarism and the growth of a revolutionary working class within Russia. Such interpretations depict the Bolsheviks as the expression of proletarian discontent, and the 'makers' of the revolution. Some Western historians, like Sheila Fitzpatrick, agree, albeit less rigidly, 'the regime was so vulnerable to any kind of jolt or setback that it is hard to imagine that it could have survived long, even without the War'.[2]

Whilst ideologically narrow Marxist interpretations have been over-taken by the fall of Communism in the 1990s, the end of Cold War certitudes similarly softened the 'Western' or 'Optimist' viewpoint. 'Optimists' argue that reformist tsarism was stabilising during the pre-war period, notwithstanding the presence of significant industrial unrest. They stress the essential placidity of the countryside, where Stolypin's reforms had created a capitalist peasant class, and the continued existence of the Duma, citing Stolypin's oft-quoted claim that, with 20 years of peace, Russia would be unrecognisable. Richard Pipes contends that the pre-war industrial unrest indicates 'the progress of labor to a more advanced economic and social status', and that it is evidence of stability, rather than crisis.[3] 'Optimists' argue that the extraordinary strains of the war, and especially the experience of defeat, fatally destabilised the Russian state and thus the war was primarily responsible for the fall of tsarism. The October Revolution is portrayed as a tragic coup against a potentially liberal-democratic regime by professional revolutionaries, with minimal popular involvement or support.

Although these two schools represent opposite interpretative poles, there is broad agreement that the First World War placed the entire infrastructure of Russian government, the economy and society under intense pressure. At the Front, Russian armies were gradually driven back by the Germans, although they enjoyed some success against Austria-Hungary. At home, the economy strained to deliver the materiel required for 'Total War'. The year 1915 witnessed a disastrous shortage of muni-tions at the Front (although Norman Stone points out that huge stockpiles existed in fortresses to the rear).[4] Munitions production recovered after the creation of War Industries Committees in 1915, and by 1917 there were substantial reserves. However, the requirements of the Home Front were neglected; textiles production, for example, collapsed, and consequently prices rose by an estimated 600 per cent by 1917. Overloading of the transport system resulted in all available resources being diverted to war supplies, leaving the cities unable to maintain regular deliveries of food. Power cuts, lengthening hours and falling wages accentuated the discontent of the urban population. The peasantry were equally unhappy, since the transportation difficulties and the absence of consumer goods made it neither possible nor in their interests to share their substantial surpluses of grain with the cities. The government was no longer trusted or respected, partly because of its manifest failures during the war, and partly because of the appearance it gave of disregard for the contributions of the people and their 'representatives' in the Duma.

Indeed, it is hard to deny the central role played by the regime in its own demise. Christopher Read has recently restated this point forcefully: 'To the very end, through its inflexibility and ineptness, the autocracy had been the principal architect of its own downfall.'[5] No one seriously entertains the conspiracy theories surrounding Alexandra and Rasputin with which tsarists consoled themselves after the catastrophe, but there is a consensus regarding the mismanagement of the country during wartime. Recent work on the secret police and the industrial establishment has reinforced the impression that the increasingly desperate efforts of industrialists, soldiers, politicians and policemen to save tsarism were constantly undermined by the central government.[6]

Consequently Russia entered 1917 on the verge of revolution, which virtually everyone except the Tsar and his entourage saw coming. The French ambassador observed that 'anything is preferable to the state of anarchy that characterises the present situation. I am obliged to report that, at the present moment, the Russian Empire is run by lunatics',[7] and the Okhrana reported that 'an abyss is opening between the masses and the government'. At an armaments conference in Petrograd, Allied delegates were dismayed to find Russian ministers openly squabbling. Behind the scenes, Duma leaders, generals, and worried aristocrats conspired to remove Nicholas and replace him with a 'strong-man' who would lead the country to victory in the war. In the end, however, it was not the conspirators, the Duma, or the handful of professional revolutionaries who overthrew the Tsar. It was the ordinary people of Petrograd, whose desperate economic situation drove them into an increasingly hostile stance towards the regime. Historians have stressed the overwhelmingly economic nature of worker protests. During the last months of the tsarist regime, 92 per cent of Moscow strikes were economic,[8] which substantiates Smith's assertion that 'the revolutionary process of 1917 can only be understood in the context of a growing crisis of the economy'.[9] The failure of the government to adequately address the workers' demands for political and civil rights and economic reform, led the WICs to become more militant. Forty per cent of Petrograd's workforce supported the demonstration marking the twelfth anniversary of Bloody Sunday on 9 January 1917, and the arrest of the leaders provoked a series of strikes demanding their release. Although the Bolsheviks and other revolutionary groups were active in this movement, it is apparent that the impetus for these protests came primarily from the workers themselves.

Nicholas, 400 miles away at army headquarters, misunderstood the meaning of this unrest, partly because the dispatches he received from his wife and ministers were relentlessly and blindly optimistic – Alexandra claimed that 'this is a hooligan movement; young people run and shout that there is no bread, simply to create excitement'.[10] The Empress, like her ministers, believed that no bread riot could result in revolution, because the real threat came from the Duma politicians. Consequently, the Tsar's orders to restore peace in the capital failed to appreciate the impossibility of doing so with disenchanted and mutinous troops. The need for last-ditch reforms to stave off revolution was never understood, despite the pleas of loyal Duma politicians like Rodzianko. Indeed, to the last, Nicholas and his advisers regarded the very people who were trying to save him as the leaders of the unrest!

In fact, there were no leaders. Notwithstanding the re-formation of the Petrograd Soviet and the 'Provisional Committee of the Duma', or the role played by newspapers like *Isvestiya*, the February Revolution was accomplished by 'the street'. It was 'a spontaneous outbreak', brought about by the 'manifest inequality' of Russian society and the 'privations of war'.[11] The 'leaders' stepped in only at the last moment to circumscribe the revolution, forcing the abdication of the Romanovs and, reluctantly, setting up a revolutionary government to restore order.

However, the new government was weakened from the outset by its relationship with the Soviet. Although the two bodies collaborated over various reforms, including the establishment of free speech, an eight-hour working day and the abolition of the death penalty, some historians have argued that deep-seated differences regarding the continuation of the war led the Soviet from the outset to seek to undermine the government. The issuing of 'Order Number 1' and the Soviet's call for an end to the war would seem to support such a view.

Between March and September, the new government attempted to establish the first parliamentary regime in Russian history. However, the Provisional Government was hopelessly divided and prone to in-fighting. The resignations of Miliukov and Gutchkov in May, and repeated walkouts by the Kadets, left the regime looking increasingly fragile and narrow-based. Moreover the decision to continue the war, whilst understandable, virtually guaranteed that the regime would fail in its task. The problems that had brought the Tsar down – military defeat, inflation, industrial unrest, growing rural discontent and the absence of civil liberties and genuine popular involvement in government – were too great to be addressed during wartime. Indeed, the war only exacerbated them. War-weariness had been the undoing of the old regime, and gradually the failure of the Provisional Government to end the war eroded its authority too, driving a deep wedge between government and people.

Furthermore, the new government made a number of important errors. A political amnesty issued in March resulted in the return of hard-line revolutionaries like Lenin, who immediately called for an acceleration of the revolutionary process, declared 'no support for the Provisional Government' and demanded the nationalisation of industry and landed estates. The 'Land Question' became increasingly problematical, as rural areas became more and more detached from the cities, and the peasants became increasingly alienated. Although the Provisional Government promised the redistribution of noble and tsarist estates after the end of the war, this simply set off peasant disturbances, as villagers forced the pace of land redistribution, encouraged by Bolshevik and left-wing Social Revolutionary agitators.

The disastrous Kerensky Offensive provoked anti-war demonstrations and the July Days, yet the government's victory over the Left was undermined by Kornilov's conservative counter-revolutionary coup in August. Kerensky's decision to release Leftists and Bolsheviks from jail, arm them and organise them into a Red Guard which defeated Kornilov, enabled the Bolsheviks to escape the consequences of July. Paradoxically, the Kornilov Revolt convinced many in Petrograd that the Provisional Government was incapable of preventing counter-revolution. By September, the Bolsheviks had recruited 170,000 members and held many of the key posts in the Factory Committees and Soldiers' Soviets.

By October, the government had effectively ceased to function. Relations between the parties had broken down. Military failure at the Front had resulted in an inexorable German advance, and mass desertion. The countryside was out of control. Inflation (112 per cent between February and June) was twice the rate of wage increases (53 per cent). Lockouts and closures of factories were increasingly common. Between February and June, 100,000 workers were laid-off, yet Skobelev, the Menshevik Minister for Labour, proposed increasing the employers' freedom to hire and fire. This simply drove the factory workers more firmly into the Bolsheviks' arms. 'There was in fact no need for the Bolsheviks to go to the streets – the streets began to come to the Bolsheviks.'[12] The disintegration of the Provisional Government was evident in Kerensky's ineffectual attempts to organise resistance to the Bolsheviks when, on the night of the 25–26 October, the government was overthrown.

The February Revolution occurred because a feeble and inefficient regime with little public sympathy failed to cope with an enormous challenge which Russia was insufficiently modernised, economically and politically, to overcome. Russia entered a deep political and economic crisis in August 1914; the material resources of the country were stretched to breaking point, and the antiquated political and administrative systems governing the state were unable to respond to the demands placed upon them. The personnel at the top of the system proved utterly inadequate to the task of guiding Russia through these desperate times, and consequently, by February 1917, the system was near to collapse. Recent analyses of the fall of tsarism have tended to focus on the failures of the administrative and political system, rather than the economy. Bulgakov argues 'the reasons for the Russian army's defeat were not just to do with quantities of guns, men, resources and foodstuffs. The fact was that the old regime was incapable of waging a modern total war.'[13] This incapacity prepared the ground for the revolutions of 1917. Throughout all analyses of the fall of tsarism, the destabilising impact of 'Total War' runs as a constant thread. The continuation of the war under tsarism's liberal successors resulted almost inevitably in the second revolution of 1917. In effect the wartime crisis that enveloped Russia in 1914 destroyed both regimes.

Questions

1. To what extent was tsarism responsible for its own downfall in February 1917?
2. How far was the war the primary reason for the fall of both the tsarist regime and Provisional Government?

ANALYSIS (2): WHY DID THE FIRST WORLD WAR RESULT IN THE FALL OF THE REGIME IN GERMANY?

If the war was a significant factor in the fall of the Romanovs in Russia, then it has been seen by historians as the predominant reason for the fall of the Hohenzollern dynasty in Germany. The collapse of Germany in 1918 was so sudden and spectacular that the causes of the ensuing revolution have generally been sought in the events of the First World War, and the social, economic and political pressures which accompanied it. Certainly these pressures were very great.

The war strained every sinew of the German economy beyond breaking point. Notwithstanding Paul Kennedy's observation that the achievement of Germany, in fighting such a long and demanding war against a coalition vastly superior in economic, financial and manpower terms, was indeed remarkable,[14] the strain of this undertaking had, by 1918, ground down both German industry and German society. In 1918, serious labour shortages disrupted German industry, despite the influx of women into the workplace, the implementation of the Hindenburg Programme and the use of prisoners of war and slave labour from occupied Europe. At this crucial juncture, the military was forced to release thousands of skilled workers from front-line duties in order to ensure continued production of essential materials. Consequently, the Hindenburg Programme effectively resulted in increasingly desperate manpower shortages at the Front, which would prove critical in the failure of the 1918 offensives. During the 1918 campaigns, the German army could only deploy four fifths of the manpower available to the Western Allies, and the Allied superiority in artillery, machine guns and, crucially, tanks would prove decisive for the first time.

Furthermore, the huge demands of the Hindenburg Programme were made at a time when the workforce were suffering from an inadequate food supply and declining nutrition. During 1918, Germany suffered more civilian deaths than in all the other years of the war combined, her people enduring desperate food shortages and surviving on less than 2,000 calories per day. The food supply reached a new nadir in August, just as the German army at the Front began to fall back, and this combination of factors further undermined morale and the will to resist. At a War Cabinet meeting in October 1918, Scheidemann argued that 'The lengthy war has already broken the spirit of the people. . . . We have no more meat. Potatoes cannot be delivered because we are short four thousand cars every day. . . . The distress is so great that one . . . asks "How does North Berlin live and how does East Berlin live?" As long as this puzzle cannot be solved, it is impossible to improve morale.'[15] As morale on the Home Front evaporated, German propaganda, unlike that of her enemies in the West, could offer no promises of a better future, instead emphasising sacrifice and duty. Such appeals increasingly fell upon deaf ears.

In political terms, the Hindenburg Programme failed to reconcile the competing demands of the entrepreneurs, for less regulation and state intervention, with those of the workers, for more and more effective intervention. Whereas before the war both groups would have regarded one another as their chief enemies, this administrative failure drew the fire of both workers and industrialists down upon the state and its bureaucracy, who generally received the blame for every perceived ill during the war. Farmers complained that price ceilings were set too low; the workers and hard-pressed *Mittelstand* (middle class) that they were too high. One military report on public morale observed, in 1917, that 'the population's confidence in official measures and statements is disappearing',[16] and in August 1918 the Frankfurt district reported that 'confidence in the government among workers and large sections of the Mittelstand is fast disappearing'.[17]

In essence, it was the corrosive effects of poverty and shortages, combined with the unrelenting suffering of the civilian population and the bad news from the Front, which eroded their support for the regime. The black market flourished, amongst those who could afford it. Amongst those who could not, the desperate food situation drove even the most law-abiding of citizens to evade and bypass official regulations and rationing. One union official complained, 'we all live from the black market, because otherwise we would starve'.[18] In a traditionally law-abiding culture, there was deeply felt resentment at being forced to resort to such illegalities to live, and this did much to undermine the legitimacy of the regime which inflicted such humiliations upon its people. For the bulk of the population, 'hamsterfahren' to the countryside, to obtain illegally supplies of fresh food, bread and eggs, were increasingly common, despite the regular checks conducted by police and officials on trains between cities and rural districts. Worryingly, by 1917, army intelligence reported 'daily plundering expeditions by train to the country, where food has been carted off in great quantities either through persuasion or through force',[19] and official powerlessness in the face of this is demonstrated in the fact that, in May 1918, another district reported that 'in the neighbourhood of the cities, groups of 50 to 100 persons descend on the fields, and the farmers are powerless to stop them'.[20] The state, in failing to provide for its citizens during the war, lost its legitimacy in the eyes of the workers and the *Mittelstand*. The revolution of 1918 can be seen in these terms as a function of the collapse of state authority during wartime, brought about by the special circumstances of the war. 'The state lost the psychological war, by its own mistakes, and in turn lost the right to rule.'[21]

On the political front, the war first shattered the Burgfriede and then drove a widening wedge between the OHL-dominated government and the MSPD-led Reichstag, where a broad Centre–Left coalition of disillusioned parties strove unsuccessfully from 1917 onwards to force the regime to open negotiations for a 'just' peace. The last year of the war witnessed a succession of chancellors and foreign ministers attempting to rally the support of the political nation behind the war whilst keeping their patrons in the OHL happy, a balancing act with little hope of success.

Even so, the collapse of the German state happened so suddenly in the autumn of 1918 that we would be foolish to understress the importance of military defeat. Despite the growing social tensions and discontent in Germany as the war progressed, there was no indication that the regime itself was under threat until September 1918. Indeed, the victory over Russia in the early months of 1918 had fostered a transient hope that Germany might yet win the conflict, and this had strengthened the popularity of the OHL. The success of the short-lived Fatherland Party, which gathered more than a million subscribers during autumn and winter 1917–18, suggests continued support amongst the German people for the military leadership, even if the politicians and bureaucrats were under attack.

With victory over the Russians, 3.5 million men were gathered in the west by Ludendorff to launch a decisive blow before the arrival of the US army. However 1.5 million had to be left in the east to control the newly seized land. On 21 March 1918, the Germans, using new 'stormtrooper' tactics, broke through Allied lines and captured 30 miles of territory. A further attack on 27 May took the German army to the Marne, as it had done in September 1914. However, the arrival of the Americans and the use of new British tanks prevented any further advance, and in August the Allied armies broke through the German lines, and thus began the final phase of the war, as the German army fell back and her allies, sensing that the war was lost, sued for peace. By September even the OHL could see that Germany had lost the war. There seems little doubt that, had the offensives of 1918 been successful, the heady experience of victory would have dampened any revolutionary ardour amongst the population. However, the offensives were, we can see with hindsight, extremely unlikely to succeed, given Germany's military, economic and manpower inferiority by 1918. If anything, the do-or-die campaigns of 1918 accelerated the collapse of the German state, by bringing the economy and the army to their knees.

Indeed, contrary to the 'stab-in-the-back' myth fostered by the propagandists of the OHL after the war's end, the army at the front line disintegrated during 1918, without any assistance from Ludendorff's mythical Red activists. As early as 1916, officials in Saxony had reported that 'discord is also not infrequently sown by the troops on leave and their accounts of life at . . . the front'.[22] After the breakdown of Ludendorff's offensive in 1918, desertions became more common (some contemporaries and historians have estimated that they numbered 200,000 or more); mutinies occurred amongst troops sent to the Front; and upwards of 750,000 soldiers sought ways to avoid fighting, through self-inflicted wounds or disciplinary offences which resulted in detention.[23]

Thus, as defeat became inevitable, German society, both civilian and military, parted company with the state. The regime which had taken Germany into the war and which had governed throughout the conflict had patently failed, and, just as importantly, the values which it rested upon had been fatally undermined by the experience of war. In these respects the First World War can be seen as the predominant factor bringing about the German Revolution in 1918.

Kocka and Feldman[24] have argued, however, that the roots of the 1918 revolution can nonetheless be traced back to pre-existing tensions before 1914, not between the state and the people, but between the industrial middle classes and the workers. That the revolution took the limited, explicitly political form of 1918 is explained by the short-lived alliance formed in the autumn of 1918 by the representatives of both of these groups, the employers and the unions. This was founded upon the concessions granted through the Hindenburg Programme, whereby labour leaders had co-operated in the suppression of workplace rights in return for recognition of the unions as partners in the administration of wartime government. This co-operative relationship, however artificial, provided a template upon which employers and labour leaders could open negotiations during autumn 1918, when defeat and revolution stared Germany in the face. The resulting 'Stinnes-Legien agreement', signed on 12 November 1918, cemented, albeit briefly, an unlikely alliance between employers and workers' representatives, ensuring the democratisation of the regime in October, whilst preserving the industrialists and their interests in the face of the German Revolution. The decision of the OHL to sponsor a 'revolution from above' in September 1918, with the aim of surviving the imminent upheaval intact and, in the future, reasserting their control over the German state (as Ludendorff put it, 'later one hopes to swing into the saddle again and rule according to the old prescription'), was the military's equivalent of this arrangement.

The acceptance by the elites of democratic reforms in September/October 1918 took the wind out of the sails of the workers' political representatives, the MSPD and the unions, and thereby undermined the forthcoming revolution, ensuring that the events of November resulted only in very limited political and social-economic changes. Having celebrated this unlikely marriage, the combined weight of the workers and the employers was turned on the administrative and political apparatus, represented most visibly (if inaccurately) by the Kaiser, who ended up bearing the brunt of the blame for the suffering of the war. Thus, pre-war social tensions were channelled into a cul-de-sac – the removal of the political leadership and the institution of limited political reform, whilst maintaining the existing social structure and many of the existing political institutions.

Whilst Kocka and Feldman's analysis of the revolutionary events of 1918 carries considerable weight, the pursuit of the longer-term roots of the upheaval back into pre-war Germany is only partially satisfying. Without denying the existence of social tensions and unresolved political and constitutional questions in pre-war Germany, the essentially unrevolutionary mood of German society before the war seems unarguable. Consequently, it seems that the explanation for the spectacular collapse of the German regime in 1918 needs to be sought in the failure of the wartime government to successfully balance the needs of the military with those of the civilian population, and in the final defeat of the German military during 1918, which provided an opportunity for the gathering discontent amongst Reichstag critics, under-nourished citizens and war-weary front-line soldiers to find expression.

Questions

1. When and why did the Kaiser's abdication become unavoidable?
2. Did the Second Reich collapse simply because of the First World War?

SOURCES

1. THE COLLAPSE OF THE GERMAN AND RUSSIAN ARMIES

Source A: General Krymov on the state of the Russian army.

The spirit of the army is such that news of a coup would be welcomed with joy. A revolution is imminent and we at the Front feel it to be so. If you decide on such an extreme step, we will support you. Clearly there is no other way.

Source B: a historian assesses the condition of the Russian army in 1917.

Among the troops destructive forces were quietly at work. Desertions assumed massive proportions: Grand Duke Sergei . . . estimated early in January 1917 that 1 million or more soldiers had shed their uniforms and returned home. There were problems with military discipline. By 1916, most of the professional officers had fallen in battle or retired because of wounds. . . . These had been replaced with freshly commissioned personnel . . . on whom the troops, especially combat veterans, looked with disdain. Instances occurred of officers refusing to lead troops into combat for fear of being shot by them.

Source C: ministerial report on the state of the Russian army, December 1916.

The army in the rear and at the fighting line is full of elements, some of whom may become an active force of rebellion, while others may refuse to participate in punitive measures against the mutineers. Should the former succeed in organising themselves properly, there would hardly be enough units in the Army to constitute a strong counter-revolutionary force to defend the government.

Source D: the Spa Conference, 29 September 1918, described by the German Foreign Secretary, Admiral Paul Von Hintze.

General Ludendorff explained the military situation .... The condition of the army required immediate ceasefire in order to avert a catastrophe ...

As a means I mentioned:

1. Dictatorship ... tied to the condition that military successes, if not victory, could be promised in the near future ...
2. Revolution from above .... Unleash a people's war, which would send every last man to the front .... Let the broadest circles be given an interest in the outcome by drawing them into the government ...
3. An invitation to conclude peace via the President of the United States, on the basis of published proposals ...

General Ludendorff rejected dictatorship: victory would be impossible, the state of the army demanded rather an immediate ceasefire. The Field Marshal and General Ludendorff approved the revolution from above.

Source E: a historian comments on morale in the German army in 1918.

The number of deserters increased considerably after the 1918 spring offensives. On the Eastern Front the war weariness led to widespread insubordination; in one case 5,000 soldiers refused to be transported to fight in the West .... Within Germany mutinies occurred where men were ordered to the front. Soldiers tried to avoid being sent into combat and plundered shops; rowdy scenes and shooting incidents at railway stations where soldiers were passing through became alarmingly frequent .... The number of disciplinary offences sky-rocketed and Ludendorff himself spoke in July 1918 of an 'increasing incidence of unauthorised leave, acts of cowardice and refusal to follow orders in the face of the enemy on the Western Front'.

Source F: Ludendorff, interviewed in 1919, explains the defeat of 1918.

An English general said with justice 'The German Army was stabbed in the back.'

Questions

1. Why did the OHL prefer to approach the US President for a peace based on his proposals (Source D)? (3 marks)
2. How valuable is Source D to a historian studying the reasons for the German revolution of 1918? (3 marks)
3. Account for the differences between the views Ludendorff expresses in Sources D and F regarding the condition of the German army in 1918. (4 marks)
*4. To what extent do Sources B and C support the view expressed by Krymov that 'news of a coup would be welcomed with joy' by the Russian army in 1917? (5 marks)
5. Using all the Sources and your own knowledge, assess the extent to which the German and Russian revolutions were a result of military defeat. (10 marks)

Worked answer

*4. *[In this question you are asked to validate the claim made in Source A with reference to the other specified extracts. It does not require the deployment of any external knowledge, but you should apply your understanding of the context of these sources to help you to evaluate them, and to derive the implicit content. This answer can be dealt with in two paragraphs, summarising in turn the extent to which the claim is corroborated or contradicted.]*

Krymov's claim that the Russian army would welcome a coup against the Tsar in 1917 is supported by extracts B and C, albeit implicitly. He clearly feels that morale is very low, and that the soldiery are discontented, and counsels the Duma, to whom his letter is addressed, that pre-emptive action to remove the source of Russia's problems is necessary to prevent revolution. His assessment is borne out by Source B. Here, the historian has assembled evidence that the Russian army had collapsed in 1917. Desertion, insubordination and even the murder of officers were undermining the fabric of the army. Desperate action would seem to have been needed in order to restore order in the ranks. Source C supports this further, in that it shows that even the notoriously ill-informed tsarist government was aware at the end of 1916 that the bulk of the army was so discontented and alienated that it would probably prove unreliable in the event of revolution.

It should be noted, however, that neither source offers explicit support for Krymov's judgement that a coup would be 'welcomed'. In fact, more than a change of government, the Russian army desired, by 1917, peace.

SOURCES

2. THE RUSSIAN AND GERMAN REVOLUTIONS

Source G: Russian Police Department Report, October 1916.

The mass of the population is at present in a very troubled mood. At the beginning of September ... an exceptional heightening of opposition and bitterness of mood became very obvious amongst wide sections of the population of Petrograd .... Towards the end of the month ... complaints were openly voiced about the venality of the government, the unbelievable burdens of the war, the unbearable conditions of everyday life. Calls from ... left wing elements on the need to 'first defeat the Germans here at home, and then deal with the enemy abroad' began to get a more and more sympathetic hearing.

In view of the fact that similar opinions are being heard at the moment in literally all sections of the population, including those which in previous years have never expressed discontent (for example certain groups of Guards officers), one cannot but share the opinion of Kadet leaders, who say, in the words of Shingarev, that 'we are very close to events of the greatest importance, in no way foreseen by the government, and which will be tragic and terrible, but are at the same time inevitable'.

Source H: report filed by a British journalist in Russia, 9 December 1916 (published in January 1917).

The most important part of the Front in Russia is undoubtedly the 'rear', for the economic disorganisation will, unless removed, interfere with further military operations .... The economic strain caused by war is beginning to make each belligerent state look more closely into its own internal condition. This is as much true of Russia as of any other belligerent .... The lack of railway facilities may be one cause which leads to this result, but perhaps more significant is the unwillingness of the government to make use of the voluntary efforts of the public bodies like the zemstvos, the Union of Cities and other popular institutions, which have shown their readiness to work for the common welfare .... Mr Miliukov, the spokesman of the Progressive Bloc in the Duma, has severely criticised the government for its attitude to the zemstvo organisations .... The Government, he said, was secretly accusing these bodies of revolutionary tendencies and was planning to 'emasculate' them.

Source I: the Tsar's own account of his abdication.

15 March, Thursday
In the morning Ruzski came and read his very long direct-wire talk with Rodzianko. According to this, the situation in Petrograd is such that a Ministry of the Duma would now be powerless to do anything. . . . My abdication is required. Ruzski transmitted this talk to Headquarters, and Alexeyev sent it on to the commanders-in-chief. By 2 o'clock replies were received from them. The gist of them is that in order to save Russia and keep the army at the front quiet, such a step must be taken. I have agreed. In the evening Gutchkov and Shulgin arrived . . . and I handed them the signed and altered manifesto. . . . All around me there is treachery, cowardice and deceit.

Source J: a German woman gives her view of the war, 1918.

Why should we work, starve, send our men out to fight? What is it all going to bring us? More work, more poverty, our men cripples, our homes ruined. What is it all for? . . . The state which called upon us to fight cannot even give us decent food.

Source K: Friedrich Ebert's view of the German Revolution.

The people were widely convinced that the Kaiser was the guilty one, and whether or not this was justified was immaterial at the present time. The main thing was that the people wanted to see the man they held responsible for the disaster removed from his post. Consequently the abdication of the Kaiser was absolutely necessary if one wanted to prevent the masses from going over to the revolutionary camp, and thus prevent revolution itself.

Questions

1. Outline the role of the following in the Russian and German revolutions:
   (i) Rodzianko (Source I). (2 marks)
   (ii) Ebert (Source K). (2 marks)
*2. Explain what is meant by the phrase 'first defeat the Germans here at home, and then deal with the enemy abroad' in Source G. (4 marks)
3. What, in your own words, does the author of Source H regard as the main cause of the February Revolution in Russia? (4 marks)
4. Identify and account for the similarities evident between Sources I and K. (5 marks)

5. Using all the Sources, and your own knowledge, consider the view that both the German and Russian regimes were responsible for their own downfall. (8 marks)

Worked answer

*2. *[This question requires that you use your own knowledge to explain the meaning of the extract. Your answer needs to be concise and very direct, whilst explaining both the specific targets of this phrase and the necessary context.]*

Amongst the rumours which circulated in Russia during the First World War was the widespread belief that the disastrous performance of the army and the state during the war was due to treason amongst the ruling elites, many of whom had German names or familial connections. This rumour tainted not only senior ministers like Sukhomlinov and Stuermer (who was unfortunate to possess a German surname) but also the Empress Alexandra, who was German by birth, and who acted as the Tsar's regent in domestic government during his absence at the Front, especially after his decision in 1915 to assume the post of Commander in Chief and move to General Headquarters (Stavka). This extract therefore reports the demands of revolutionaries for the removal of the government, smearing them with the accusation that they (specifically Alexandra and her favourite, Stuermer) were in league with the Germans.

8

VICTORY AND DEFEAT

BACKGROUND NARRATIVE

At the end of 1917, the German army and its allies were advancing on two fronts. In the east, the Russian army had collapsed and the Bolshevik revolution had brought to power a regime determined to achieve peace, whatever the cost. Negotiations for peace on the Eastern Front began in December 1917, but German territorial demands were so extensive that the Bolshevik regime dragged its feet, holding up the negotiations until the spring in the hope of a socialist revolution in Germany. By February 1918 it had become clear that this was not imminent, and a renewed German offensive, threatening Petrograd itself, forced Russia to agree to the humiliating terms of the treaty of Brest-Litovsk in March. Meanwhile, on the Italian front the Germans and Austrians broke through at Caporetto, with the Italian army in headlong retreat. As American troops began arriving in Europe, Ludendorff saw one last strategic opportunity for victory. If he could send enough troops from the East to the Western Front, a breakthrough might be achieved before 1919, when the arrival of vast numbers of American forces would lend the Allies an advantage in manpower which it would be impossible to resist.

Despite a serious shortage of manpower and materiel, the 'Ludendorff Offensive' commenced on 21 March at the junction of the British and French armies on the Somme. Using new 'stormtrooper' tactics and the element of surprise, the Germans advanced up to 50 miles in four consecutive assaults, threatening Paris as they had in 1914. Once the Allies reinforced their lines, however, the impetus of the advances was slowed and the Germans found themselves in exposed positions, having lost 500,000 of their best men without achieving a decisive breakthrough.

Exhausted and demoralised, the Germans fell back in the face of furious French attacks along the Marne which combined pinpoint artillery barrages, tank assaults, air support and infantry attacks. When the British joined the operation near Amiens on 8 August, the true state of the German army's morale was laid bare, as 30,000 troops surrendered in two days. The Allies were only able to advance slowly over the war-torn terrain, and the Germans managed to stage a coherent retreat, but the result of the war was no longer in question. On the other fronts, Germany's allies began to collapse. At the end of September, when the Allies finally broke out of Macedonia and into Serbia, the Bulgarians sued for peace. Following a major defeat at the hands of the British, the Turks surrendered on 30 October. Earlier in October, the Italians, with Allied reinforcements, broke through the Austrian lines near Vittorio Veneto. This precipitated the collapse of the Habsburg war effort, as the various ethnic groups of the Habsburg Empire abandoned the Imperial cause and raced home to secure independence for their regions. Austria-Hungary formally surrendered on 3 November.

Ludendorff finally admitted that the war was lost on 29 September, and a new, more representative Reich government sought terms for an armistice from President Wilson of the USA. Wilson insisted on the withdrawal of all German forces from occupied territory before terms would be agreed – in effect he demanded a surrender rather than an armistice. Ludendorff was unwilling to accept this and resigned on 26 October. However, faced with social revolution, the disintegration of the army and navy and the threat of invasion, the German government had no choice but to accept. Thus, on 10 November, the German Armistice Commission, led by Matthias Erzberger, representing the new German Republic, met Marshal Foch at Compiègne in France and signed the terms of the armistice. Germany agreed to evacuate all occupied territory on the Western Front, renounced the treaty of Brest-Litovsk and surrendered her surface and U-boat fleets. At 11a.m. on 11 November hostilities ceased.

ANALYSIS (1): WHY DID FRANCE AND BRITAIN DEFEAT THE CENTRAL POWERS?

The defeat of Germany and her allies was not inevitable until August 1918, but following the early failure of the Schlieffen Plan, it was always the most likely outcome. Germany, for all her tremendous efforts, possessed neither the financial nor the material resources to defeat such a large coalition of enemies, and the addition of the USA to that coalition in 1917 more than offset the loss of Russia, with the result that, in 1918, the balance tipped decisively against the Central Powers and defeat became unavoidable.

Yet, at the outset of the conflict, as Paul Kennedy has observed, Germany had seemed better equipped to wage a large modern war than her enemies.[1] Her army and navy were the most modern and efficient in the world, and her economy was, in many respects, better suited to the production of military materiel even than that of Great Britain, out-producing Britain in steel, for example. In the early days of the conflict, then, Germany possessed the advantages of greater preparedness (although even she was not really ready for 'Total War') and superior quality of arms and soldiery. These advantages were however only good for the short term, and the Schlieffen Plan indicates that the more thoughtful military minds in pre-war Germany appreciated the importance of a quick victory. Once the Schlieffen Plan had failed and the initial offensives of 1914 had ground to a halt, Germany's isolation and her inability to guarantee supplies of crucial raw materials and food hamstrung her war effort.

All the long-term advantages were possessed by Great Britain: the world's most powerful navy, her extensive overseas empire, enormous financial power and (vitally) open trade routes to Japan, the USA and the Commonwealth. The problem for Great Britain was that she was wholly unready in 1914 for 'Total War', in material, ideological and psychological terms. Britain's early contributions to the Entente's war effort were unimpressive – she never had more than 1 million men under arms at any one time[2] – and indeed the French and Russians were quick to notice this. British lassitude was a common theme of French and Russian complaints during 1915. It was 1916 before the introduction of conscription and the establishment of Lloyd George's coalition government enabled Britain to begin to mobilise her superior resources effectively, and more or less throughout the war Germany managed to squeeze more out of her economy and society than Britain did, although it may be argued that the lengths to which the German regime went to achieve this partly explain the war-weariness and discontent within Germany which culminated in revolution in 1918.

Recently, historians have turned the spotlight away from merely military explanations of the outcome of the war towards a more integrated analysis of the inter-relationship between civil society and the military. The eventual triumph of the Western Allies is now explained in terms of their greater success in balancing the needs of these two sectors, and a brief examination of the way in which the response of the belligerent states evolved as the war progressed exemplifies this. Initially, in 1914, mobilisation in every European power was largely spontaneous, a product of 'national culture', expressing itself as popular support for a war in defence of the homeland. The state did acquire new powers, but generally hesitated to deploy them at first, relying on propaganda to mobilise the nation (even here, the press, intellectuals, educationalists, churches and voluntary organisations did the lion's share of the work). In economic matters the state worked in partnership with industry to produce the necessary munitions. There were slight differences in this pattern in Russia, where the state quickly showed itself incapable of giving a lead to the war effort, partly through fear of the democratising effects of embarking on any partnership with the Duma and zemstvos politicians. This culminated in a humiliating climb-down in 1915, when the government was forced by circumstances and public pressure to accept a partnership with industry and society after all. Thus in Russia the issue of 'national mobilisation' became politicised and divisive.

Gradually, the need for total effort by state and society in order to win war, the 'totalising logic of the conflict',[3] became clear. The national myths mobilised in 1914 began to create divisions, and social solidarity was strained by evidently contrasting experiences of war. Consequently self-mobilisation had lost all its momentum by 1916. Thereafter, the state in most countries sought to assume a more central, directing role in the war effort. Conscription in Great Britain, the Hindenburg Programme in Germany, and Clemenceau's remobilisation of French society after his appointment in France in 1917, all bear witness to the state adopting a more dominant role in the organisation of the war, 're-mobilising' the nation.

However, in their response to the crises of 1916–17, the wartime regimes revealed the essence of their state systems, and this determined their ultimate fate. In Russia, the tsarist regime was simply unable to cope with criticism in any way other than with repression. However, repression deepened the gulf between state and society, and ultimately led to the February Revolution. In Germany, the Janus-like nature of the German constitution led to a choice of possible paths: authoritarian (the rule of the OHL and the Hindenburg Programme) or democratic (offered by the Reichstag in the Peace Resolution of July 1917). Those effectively in power, Hindenburg and Ludendorff, chose the former, but their critics remained, and the collapse of the Burgfriede prefigured the collapse of the German war effort. It was not possible to coerce greater commitment from the German people when their elected representatives in the Reichstag had been rebuffed and alienated from the regime. They by and large endured and complied with the requirements of the state, but the enthusiastic and whole-hearted commitment needed to make 'total mobilisation' work effectively was hereafter lacking. Amidst this declining sense of a community of interests, war-weariness took over. The sudden upsurge in strikes, mutinies and protests dates from the promulgation of the Hindenburg Programme. Even some conservatives could see by July 1917 that only credible promises of reform would rebuild the Burgfriede. In an open letter to the government in the *Berliner Tagblatt*, a group of eminent conservatives declared that 'the gigantic struggle in which the German people is engaged is not yet ended. The undersigned . . . do not hesitate publicly to emphasise the demand of the hour, namely that the German government shall forthwith lay before the Landtag franchise reforms . . . and the Government shall, in addition, give effective and definite expression to the confidence which the German people deserve.'[4] This never came. Instead the military leadership exhorted Germans to make greater sacrifices and diverted all available human and material resources to the war effort, whilst conditions on the Home Front continued to deteriorate. Wages, consumption and nutrition declined and the German non-combatant death rate during the war climbed to six times that of France (an occupied country)! Although the German people did not starve, the episodic hunger and the demoralising lengths to which ordinary citizens were forced to go in order to obtain food inexorably ground down their will to continue. 'Like an invisible net, the problems of food supply entangled German society and its leadership until the war effort became difficult, then impossible, to sustain.'[5]

By the end of 1917, the elements which would result in victory for the Western Allies and defeat for the Central Powers were in place. German finances had deteriorated, due to the reluctance of the regime to tax incomes or wartime profits, for fear of alienating their allies among the industrial elites. This 'partisan misuse of national wealth'[6] meant that Germany was reliant on inflationary policies, printing more paper money, borrowing internally and stacking up a huge national debt. But the immense demands of 'Total War' could not be financed endlessly in this manner, and by 1918 Germany was running short of money, materiel and men. The manpower shortages were critical. During the war, Germany mobilised 13.5 million men, more than any other country, and a far higher proportion of the national population than any of her rivals.

Yet the extent of the alliance ranged against her meant that she and Austria-Hungary could still call upon less than half the manpower available to her enemies. The Auxiliary Labour Law, designed to maximise the usefulness of Germany's remaining adult male population, created tremendous tensions between the needs of the front line and those of war-related industries. Over 3 million men were released from front-line duties to work in munitions-related production, but still the enormous needs of the war machine could not be met. By 1918 the Western Allies possessed huge advantages in terms of aeroplanes, tanks and trucks, and these would prove crucial during the final campaigns of the war.[7] Furthermore, the removal to industrial work of so many front-line soldiers, together with the need to garrison occupied Eastern Europe following the punitive Treaty of Brest-Litovsk which ended the war with Russia, resulted in a desperate shortage of troops on the Western Front. Germany began 1918 heavily outnumbered, and by the time Ludendorff's suicidal spring offensive had ground to a halt, Germany had sustained almost 500,000 casualties. She lost a further 1 million men by August, due to sickness, desertion and self-inflicted wounds, leaving only 2,500,000 active front-line troops.[8] The war was lost.

The military-dominated government of Germany failed to resolve its economic and military needs because of a failure to appreciate the importance of meeting the needs of its people alongside those of its military. As Winter argues, 'the waging of war, in economic matters as much as in other spheres, is essentially a political matter'.[9]

Contrast this with developments in the Western democracies. In both countries, power was wrested away from the generals and *enshrined* in coalition governments headed by populist civilian politicians, Lloyd George and Clemenceau. The British regime promised democratic reform at the end of the struggle. The French anyway were fighting to liberate their homeland from the occupying Germans and, for all their exhaustion and disaffection, they would not rest until they had done so. As the war progressed, both governments stepped up their efforts and assumed greater powers over industry and the people. The resulting experiment in 'State Capitalism' from 1915 onwards succeeded in sustaining the civilian population's standards of living, via subsidies, rent controls, separation allowances and active intervention by the state in worker–employer relations. Britain was the only country where profiteering by industrialists was even vaguely reined-in by the state, through the taxation of war profits. The state emphasised the limited nature of the nation's war aims (which contrasted with the increasingly public ambitions of the pan-Germanists inside the OHL-dominated German government). As a result of this intelligent and inclusive approach (which none the less retained room to deal with pacifists and agitators, as the Caillaux and Bertrand Russell affairs demonstrate), Britain and France balanced more effectively civilian and military needs. 'Britain and France developed a system which sustained mass armies and the populations from which they were drawn and supplied; Germany and her allies failed to do so.'[10] Therefore, when Britain and France asked for one last effort in 1918, they got it, unlike the German government later the same year. In the *crisis* of the war, democratic regimes proved more capable of demanding further sacrifices than autocratic ones. This may seem paradoxical, but as Horne notes, 'mass involvement . . . the consent of the ruled' is 'an increasingly vital condition of the state's effective operation'.[11]

To conclude, the military defeat suffered by Germany is only partly explicable in military terms. The German army performed remarkably well during the First World War, but the sheer size of the demands placed upon German society and the economy in order to meet the challenge of total war were ultimately too great to be overcome. This was true almost from the very beginning of the conflict, and it was only the extraordinary efforts of the German people and soldiery that staved off the inevitable for four years and brought their nation to what appeared to be the brink of victory during 1917. However, by this stage Germany was exhausted and, whereas Britain and France had access to overseas sources of grain and materiel, Germany, bankrupt and blockaded, was unable to draw upon such a reserve. American intervention merely reinforced this situation and hastened the end.

Eventually, as Offer asserts, the economic imbalance between the two alliances was decisive. 'Germany was not starved into defeat – nor, for that matter was it decisively beaten on the battlefield. Its downfall was ultimately a matter of economic inferiority.'[12] The German army was not, as Ludendorff and Hindenburg would later claim, 'stabbed in the back'. Neither did the front-line soldiers fail their leaders. On the contrary, the German leadership, military, political and economic, failed their people, and their defeat in significant measure resulted from this.

Questions

1. In what ways did the entry of the United States into the First World War confirm the most likely outcome of the conflict?
2. 'War is the supreme test of a country's military, social, political and economic institutions' (A. Marwick). Why did Germany fail this test?

ANALYSIS (2): HOW VALID IS THE VIEW THAT *NO* EUROPEAN POWER 'WON' THE FIRST WORLD WAR?

Whilst it is unquestionable that Germany and Russia lost the First World War, in the light of their military defeats and the economic dislocation and political violence that followed the ending of hostilities, it has been fashionable since the 1920s to argue that no European power, even the victors France and Britain, benefited sufficiently to be able to claim that they 'won' the war. This pessimistic conclusion finds most vivid expression through artistic responses to the conflict. The poetry, prose and art of World War One is dominated by the ironic and brutal aspects of the conflict, what Wilfred Owen called 'the pity of war', and these aspects have dominated all subsequent depictions of the war too. Joan Littlewood's play *Oh! What a Lovely War*, the recent novels of Pat Barker and Sebastian Faulks, films such as *Gallipoli* and even the final series of the BBC comedy *Blackadder*, focus on the atrocity of the trenches and the ignorance of the generals, to the exclusion of almost every other theme. The historian, however, must assess the impact of the war on societies, economies and empires as well as on individuals. In doing so, it is important to analyse pre-war trends in all these areas, in order accurately to evaluate the direct consequences of the war. It is by no means necessary that the changes historians have observed in the post-war world should have been effected by the war itself.

The most obvious effect of the war, it might seem, was the annihilation of an entire 'lost generation' of young men across Europe, which, as one would expect, caused the marriage and therefore the birth rate to drop, depriving the country of the leaders, managers and workforce of the future. In France, an already low birth rate declined dramatically. In 1919, the birth rate was only two-thirds what it had been in 1912, and the effects of this were evident in the 1930s, when there was only half the 'normal' number of young adults entering the workforce. The French state resorted to immigration to fill the millions of empty places in the workforce during the 1920s. However, the example of Britain (which, admittedly, suffered less heavily than the other powers)[13] suggests that the picture is in fact more complex. In common with the rest of Europe, Britain's birth rate was declining before 1914, and the reduction in this rate attributable to the war was almost made up by the post-war baby boom. After that, the birth rate continued the gradual downward spiral it had demonstrated before the war. Therefore the impact of the war on the birth rate was disruptive but not revolutionary. As for the 'lost generation', Britain had, before 1914, suffered a net loss of 200,000 people per year through emigration either to the colonies or, as with the majority of

European emigrants, to the United States. The advent of war curtailed such emigration, and it is arguable that had war not intervened Britain may have lost more of its young men to emigration than died in military conflict (although one has to concede that emigration was, by any measure, a kinder fate than death on the Western Front). The post-war imposition by the United States of restrictions on immigration, and the growth of independence movements in some of Britain's colonies, ensured that emigration remained at a much lower rate during the post-war years, and therefore the 'lost generation' was quickly replaced. This is not to argue that imbalances were not felt for many years. In 1911, there were 100 men to every 101 women. By 1925, there were 100 men to every 113 women. Unmarried women of this generation and the next put their position down to the effects of the war. The upper classes suffered a disproportionately large number of losses, as the young men from these groups tended to become front-line officers, whose survival rate, as they led their men over the top, was the worst for any rank in the armed forces.[14]

Economically, Europe was devastated by the war. Factories were destroyed, transport systems worn out or damaged, whole towns and villages were obliterated and in some areas even the soil was rendered barren. The war cost France the equivalent of 11 years of pre-war wealth accumulation. The state debt spiralled to 175 billion francs, and France lost more than 50 per cent of her overseas assets, including 12 billion francs of private and government money lost when the Soviet government repudiated their debts to foreign investors. With millions of new dependants (widows, orphans and disabled 'poilus') to support and a rising cost of living, it was not perhaps surprising that the French were unanimous in demanding that Germany should pay for the damage caused, but this issue would dangerously destabilise relations between the Third Republic and the Weimar government for the next five years. Some regions actually benefited, however, as production was stepped up or relocated to provide munitions for the war effort. 'Grenoble has become a veritable industrial centre, thanks to the tremendous efforts of our industries, merchants and workers.'[15] Meanwhile, other areas were devastated, especially those occupied by the rapacious German forces. In Lille, where German troops marched into the city on 12 October 1914, the war witnessed a dramatic fall in population from 217,000 to 112,000. Most of those who remained were the aged, women and children, but these were forced to provide more than 184 million francs for their occupiers, which left the city with a municipal debt in 1919 of more than 300 million francs. Thousands were deported to work in Germany's under-populated factories and the death rate doubled amongst the remaining civilian population, mainly due to poor nutrition.[16]

Although Britain did not suffer as much structural damage as France, her economy was equally adversely affected by the war. The 'staple industries' of textiles, coal, iron, steel and shipbuilding, on which the British economy was dangerously reliant, lost vital overseas markets, either to domestic production or US and Japanese firms. In Brazil, an important customer of the British cotton industry before the war, domestic production replaced British imports, and the Japanese cotton industry gobbled up British markets in south-east Asia.[17] Only one-third of wartime expenditure was covered by increased taxation, which had forced Britain to liquidate many of her foreign investments and to borrow heavily, especially from the USA. As a result, 'Britain was to emerge from the war a debtor nation, when before it had been a creditor.'[18] The City of London had been the hub of global financial services such as banking and insurance before the war, but, with its assets depleted, New York displaced it as the world's premier financial centre. On the other hand, the loss of German imports encouraged Britain to develop newer industries such as chemicals, electrical goods, radio, motor vehicles, and aircraft. New industrial techniques, such as standardisation, mass production and more efficient management, were introduced widely. Heavy industry enjoyed a boom, which makes one wonder, if their profits had been more wisely spent on modernising and diversifying, whether these industries would have been better able to withstand the industrial recessions of the 1920s and 1930s.

In general, Europe's historical world dominance, economic and political, was terminated by the First World War. Her share of world manufacturing production fell from 43 per cent (1913) to 34 per cent (1923), with the main beneficiary being North America, although Asia (particularly Japan) gained ground too. Europe's share of world trade showed a similar trend.[19]

At the end of the war, both the British and French Empires were at their zenith in terms of their size, as the German and Turkish colonies were dismembered and transferred (under the figleaf of League of Nations mandates) to Britain and France, despite the promise of 'self-determination'. However, given the cost of the war, neither could now afford to control and defend this enormous portion of the earth, especially as the war had caused many rural peoples in the colonies to move into cities where they became increasingly conscious of nationalist movements, such as those of Gandhi in India and the Wafd party in Egypt. Britain also had responsibility for two of the most bitterly divided areas of the world – Palestine and Ireland – and her decision to grant autonomy to the south of Ireland in 1922 demonstrated the 'imperial overstretch' that she was suffering. That move made the situation worse in some ways, however, as nationalists elsewhere attempted to follow the Irish Free

State's example, and Britain and France oscillated between repression and reform in order to contain the problem. Furthermore, they both had to defend these troublesome areas from external threat as well, which may well go some way to explain their reluctance to confront the aggression of Mussolini and Hitler during the inter-war years, as the difficulties of defending their Far East possessions from militant Japan were felt to be more pressing than the problems in Central and Eastern Europe.

Throughout Europe, workers (at least those who survived) made significant gains during the war as real wages increased, and both the trade unions and the socialist parties emerged stronger in 1918 than they had been in 1914. French workers were granted the eight-hour maximum day, as well as a Housing Act in 1922, which provided cheap government loans and subsidies for working-class, pensioners' and war victims' housing. In Britain, unemployment insurance was extended to cover nearly all workers in 1920 and a Ministry of Health was established in 1919. These and other wartime gains, which marked a distinct break from pre-war attitudes towards welfare provision, led to further demands for more improvements such as better pay and conditions, improved education and more housing. The state's capacity to direct, intervene and improve had been confirmed by the war, and a large proportion of the population of Europe believed that this power could continue to be used to remedy social injustices after the war. However, it is equally true to say that the middle classes, who had suffered disproportionately high death rates and, for those on fixed incomes especially, a decline in their standard of living, now became more determined to resist these demands. They believed, quite correctly, that they would have to fund such improvements through higher taxes. Therefore the political legacy of the war, was, for both Britain and France, as well as Germany and Russia, heightened inter-class antagonism, rather than the mythical cross-class camaraderie that was supposedly encouraged in the trenches. In Britain this led to the inter-war dominance of the Conservatives, the formation of the Middle Class Union, and organised opposition to the General Strike. After a brief flurry of bitter industrial conflict between workers and bosses during 1919–20, French political life returned to the pre-war pattern and atmosphere, with a rapid succession of Prime Ministers but little change in the governing 'Bloc National' coalition in the immediate post-war years. Hopes for the modernisation of the political system proved short-lived, and there seems to have been little real demand for reform, rather a yearning for a return to a (largely mythical) pre-war stability. This was finally located in a broad coalition, headed by Poincaré, which governed from 1926. Elsewhere in Europe, where the fear of acquisitive socialism and Bolshevism was heightened by terrible economic hardship, many middle-class voters rejected 'feeble' democratic parties altogether and put their trust in right-wing extremists. Sadly for them, having handed power to such groups, they were unable to stop them starting a Second World War and thus returning Europe to plunder, famine and murder and the eventual triumph of Soviet Communism in half of Europe.

In geo-political terms, as George Kennan observed in 1979, the First World War was '*the* seminal catastrophe of this century'.[20] Germany's treatment at Versailles failed to deprive her completely of the ability to wage war, yet gave her a number of strong reasons to do so. The emergence of a regime antithetical to capitalism in Soviet Russia began a period of global competition that only ended in 1989, and the economic dominance of the USA was accelerated and confirmed. If Britain and France *lost* the war, it was because they failed to understand this geo-political development and attempted to return to a pre-war 'golden age' of imperial and economic domination. Too late, they discovered that the war had rendered them incapable of fulfilling such a role, and it took a second war to convince the majority of Europeans, and prolonged economic decline to convince the British, that European co-operation was the only means for small nation states to prosper in the 'new world order'.

Questions

1. How stable were the British and French Empires in 1918?
2. Did the scale of death and suffering in the First World War inhibit the subsequent foreign policies of Britain and France?

SOURCES

1. THE DEFEAT OF THE CENTRAL POWERS

Source A: industrial and technological comparison of the alliances in 1914 and 1917.

	Germany/Austria	France, Britain, Russia (1914–17)	France, Britain, USA (1917 onwards)
% output of world manufacturing	19.2%	27.9%	57.7%
Energy consumption	236.4 million tons	311.8 million tons	798.8 million tons
Steel production	20.2 million tons	17.1 million tons	44.1 million tons
Industrial potential (UK 1900 = 100)	178.4	261.1	472.6

Source B: the war effort, 1914–18.

	War expenditure	Mobilised forces
Great Britain	$23 billion	9.5 million
France	$9.3 billion	8.2 million
Russia	$5.4 billion	13.0 million
Other Allies (inc USA)	$20 billion	12.0 million
Allied forces	$57.7 billion	40.7 million men
Germany	$19.9 billion	13.25 million
German allies	$4.8 billion	11.85 million
Central Powers	$24.7 billion	25.10 million men

Source C: material resources, early 1918.

	Germany (Western forces)	Western Allies
Machine guns (per division)	324	1,084
Artillery	c. 14,000	c. 18,500
Aeroplanes	c. 3,670	c. 4,500
Trucks	23,000	c. 100,000
Tanks	10	800

Source D: the Zimmermann Telegram to the German Ambassador in Mexico, as released to the US press, March 1917.

We intend to begin unrestricted submarine warfare on the first day of February. We shall endeavour in spite of this to keep the United States neutral. In the event of this not succeeding, we make Mexico a proposal of alliance on the following basis: Make war together, generous financial support, and an understanding on our part that Mexico is to reconquer the lost territory in Texas, New Mexico and Arizona . . .

Source E: a historian, John Williams, comments on some of the reasons for Germany's defeat.

The single most important element in maintaining civilian morale was sufficiency of food. The most glittering military successes counted for little against an unsatisfied stomach. Second only to food was warmth. The lack of these two basic needs (besides obviously impairing the physical vitality and productive power of the workers) sapped, like nothing else, the spirit and will to carry on.

Source F: a historian, Roger Chickering, analyses the reasons for the war's outcome.

The fateful moments of the war came at the first hour, when the British intervened in the continental conflict, and then in early 1917, when the United States formally joined the coalition arrayed against the Central Powers. The British intervention was pivotal. Apart from ensuring the commitment of British troops and material resources to the coalition, it turned the commercial balance to the decisive disadvantage of the Central Powers, which were, for all intents and purposes, denied access to overseas trade for the duration of the war. The western powers, by contrast, henceforth enjoyed privileged access to the resources of the world's most formidable industrial power. Agricultural imports from America likewise spared the western powers from food shortages in the degree that plagued the Central Powers. The German decision to risk war with the United States in 1917 ... sealed the eventual defeat of the Central Powers, for it led to the acceleration and expansion of the American commitment of financial, material and human resources to the war against Germany.

Questions

*1. (i) Who was 'Zimmermann' (Source D)? (1 mark)
    (ii) What was the outcome of the publication of the Zimmermann Telegram (Source D) in the US press? (2 marks)
2. Comment on what Source A tells us about the balance of economic strength between the two alliance systems in 1914. (4 marks)
3. To what extent might Sources A and B be used to explain the situation described in Source C? (5 marks)
4. Identify and explain the similarities and differences between the analyses given in Sources D and E. (5 marks)
5. Using all the Sources, and your own knowledge, consider the view that the defeat of the Central Powers was primarily brought about by their relative economic weakness. (8 marks)

Worked answer

*1. (i) Zimmermann was the German Foreign Minister in January 1917, at the time when the Zimmermann Telegram was dispatched.
*1. (ii) The result of the interception and publication of the Zimmermann Telegram was to lever the Americans into joining the war on the Western Allies' side. Although it was likely that this would have

occurred anyway, as the full effects of unrestricted submarine warfare were felt upon neutral US shipping, the telegram was important in swinging US public opinion and the support of Congress behind President Wilson's decision to enter the war.

SOURCES

2. THE LEGACY OF THE WAR

Source G: casualty figures for the European Great Powers.

	Total of mobilised forces	Killed and died	Total casualties*	Total casualties as % of total mobilised
Russia	12,000,000	1,700,000	9,150,000	76.3%
France	8,410,000	1,357,800	6,160,800	73.3%
British Empire	8,904,467	908,371	3,190,235	35.8%
Germany	11,000,000	1,773,700	7,142,558	64.9%
Total of all combatant countries	65,038,810	8,538,315	37,494,186	57.6%

*Total casualties includes prisoners, wounded and missing

Source H: world indices of manufacturing production, 1913–25.

	1913	1920	1925
World	100	93.6	121.6
Europe*	100	77.3	103.5
USSR	100	12.8	70.1
USA	100	122.2	148.0
Rest of world	100	109.5	138.1

*(excluding USSR)

Source I: from 'The Policy of France' by A. Tardieu, 1922.

The financial consequences of the annihilations of all [our] resources bear down on us heavily today. The war cost us 150 billions of francs. The damage to property and persons comes to 200 billions. Our ordinary budget has increased from 4.5 billions to 25 billions; our debt from 36 billions to 330 billions. Since the armistice we have spent on reconstruction and pensions a total of 90 billions and we have received from Germany in one form or another, less than two billions of gold marks (about six billions of francs) or about six per cent of what we have had to spend on restoring our provinces − a task as yet but half completed.

Source J: Paul Kennedy on the after-effects of the war.

To hundreds of thousands of former *Frontsoldaten* across the continent of Europe, disillusioned by the unemployment and inflation and boredom of the post-war bourgeois-dominated order, the conflict had represented something searing, but positive; martial values, the camaraderie of warriors, the thrill of violence and action. To such groups, especially in the defeated nations of Germany and Hungary, but also among the French right, the ideas of the new fascist movements − of order, discipline, and national glory, of the smashing of the Jews, Bolsheviks, intellectual decadents, and self-satisfied liberal middle classes − had great appeal. In their eyes (and in the eyes of their equivalents in Japan) it was struggle and force and heroism, which were the enduring features of life, and the tenets of Wilsonian internationalism which were false and outdated.

Source K: 'The Dead Statesman' by Rudyard Kipling, 1918.

I could not work: I dared not rob
Therefore, I lied to please the mob.
Now all my lies are proved untrue
And I must face the men I slew.
What tale shall serve me here among
Mine angry and defrauded young?

Source L: from 'The Consequences of the War to Great Britain' by F.W. Hirst.

Levelling was inevitable in a period when a duke's son served under his gardener's boy; or a duke's daughter hoed turnips while her 'social superiors' were buying themselves fur coats out of their earnings in the munition factories. It is significant that you seldom hear nowadays the phrase which was once so common: 'I know my station'.

Questions

1. In light of Source G, assess the relative damage suffered by the European Great Powers. (4 marks)

2. Which long-term economic consequences of the Great War are identified in Source H? (4 marks)
3. How well justified is the demand for German reparations in Source I, considering the evidence in Sources G and H? (6 marks)
4. How adequately does Source J explain Kipling's poem (Source K)? (5 marks)
*5. Did the attitude expressed in Source K lead to the change in social relations described in Source L? (6 marks)

Worked answer

*5. Source K's attitude towards statesmen, members of Britain's social elite, would seem to confirm the diminution of respect towards 'social superiors' described in Source L. However, it is worth remembering that Kipling, whose only son, John, died in the war, may be expressing a personal reaction directed at those politicians who he felt were guilty of causing and prolonging a war in which so many 'young' died. On the other hand, Kipling, a rich and successful man himself, was popularly regarded as the 'bard of empire' in the pre-war years and the bitterness of the poem may well be partly aimed at himself, as well as those other leading cultural and political figures who popularised an assertive British foreign policy, which helped to cause British involvement in the Great War.

It is worth noting, however, that Source L tends to exaggerate the change in social relations caused by the war. The incidents of inverted class relations described in the Source were popular hearsay during the war, widely disseminated by newspapers and journals whose motive was to maintain national unity as the unprecedented death toll mounted. The predominance of the upper classes among the officer ranks of the armed forces, and the almost uniformly working-class composition of the Women's Land Army, mean that such incidents were either non-existent or so rare as to be of no significance. It may well be true to say that women munition workers and the working class generally enjoyed a better level of real wages than before the war, but to say that they were able to buy fur coats is both inaccurate and patronising. As the post-war years showed, although the outward signs of deference may have become less prevalent, the dominance of the Conservative Party in an age of full democracy intimated that popular respect for 'social superiors' was by no means dead.

Therefore, it is perhaps best to see Kipling's poem as part of the wave of anti-war sentiment that emerged in literature in the late 1920s. This reflected the revulsion for war felt by many, once the benefits of the war had been assessed and found to be few. Part of that revulsion was aimed at the people held responsible for the war, but it is an over-simplification to state that this directly led to change in social relations in Britain or elsewhere.

NOTES

INTRODUCTION

1 See J. Winter and J.-L. Robert (eds): *Capital Cities at War: London, Paris, Berlin, 1914–1919* (Cambridge 1997), introduction.
2 See E. Hobsbawm: *Age of Extremes: The Short Twentieth Century 1914–1991* (London 1995).

1. THE OUTBREAK OF WAR

1 See F. Fischer: *Germany's Aims in the First World War* (London 1967).
2 P. Kennedy: *The Rise and Fall of the Great Powers* (London 1989), pp. 270–1.
3 W.B. Lincoln: *Passage through Armageddon: The Russians in War and Revolution* (Oxford 1986), p. 133.
4 Quoted in N. Stone: *The Eastern Front* (London 1975), p. 37.
5 Col. A. Knox: *With the Russian Army, 1914–1917* (London 1921), p. 32.
6 A.J.P. Taylor: *English History 1914–1945* (Oxford 1965), p. 8.
7 J.F. Godfrey: *Capitalism at War* (Leamington Spa 1987), pp. 46–7.
8 Quoted in H. Rogger: *Russia in the Age of Modernisation and Revolution, 1881–1917* (London 1983), p. 255.
9 Quoted in W.B. Lincoln: op. cit., p. 45.
10 Quoted in H. Rogger: op. cit., p. 256.
11 See E.H.H. Green: *The Crisis of Conservatism* (London 1995), ch. 11.
12 Quoted in D. Murphy *et al.*: *Britain 1815–1918* (London 1998), p. 312.
Source A: J. Kocka: *Facing Total War* (Leamington Spa 1984), p. 12.
Source B: H. Cowper *et al.*: *World War One and Its Consequences* (Buckingham 1990), p. 109.

Source C: C. Trebilcock: *The Industrialisation of the Continental Powers* (London 1981), p. 443.

Source D: M. Lynch: *Reaction and Revolutions: Russia 1881–1924* (London 1989), p. 24.

Source E: ibid.

Source F: T. Kemp: *Industrialisation in 19th Century Europe* (London 1969), p. 203.

Source G: (i) C. Trebilcock: op. cit., p. 450; (ii) P. Kennedy: op. cit., p. 255.

Source H: P. Kennedy: op. cit., p. 300–1.

Source I: quoted in A.J. Plotke (ed.): *Great War Primary Document Archive*. Brigham Young University. Online. Available HTTP: http://www.lib.byu.edu/~rdh/wwi/ (29 June 1999).

Source J: quoted in M. Shevin-Coetzee and F. Coetzee: *World War One and European Society: A Sourcebook* (Lexington 1995), pp. 29–30.

Source K: quoted in A.J. Plotke: op. cit.

Source L: quoted in ibid.

Source M: quoted in A. Marwick: *War and Social Change in the Twentieth Century* (London 1974), p. 33.

2. RECRUITMENT AND PROPAGANDA

1 C. Haste: *Keep the Home Fires Burning: Propaganda in the First World War* (London 1977), p. 84.

2 A. Mendelssohn-Bartholdy: *The War and German Society* (New Haven 1937).

3 See J. Lawrence: 'Transition to War in 1914' in J. Winter and J.-L. Robert (eds): op. cit.

4 See J. Horne (ed.): *State, Society and Mobilization in Europe during the First World War* (Cambridge 1997), introduction.

5 Quoted in A. Marwick: *The Deluge* (London 1965), p. 53.

6 Quoted in G. J. de Groot: *Blighty: British Society in the Era of the Great War* (London 1996), p. 93.

7 See P. Simkins: *Kitchener's Army: The Raising of the New Armies 1914–1916* (Manchester 1988).

8 Ibid., p. 106.

9 See W. Coupe: 'German Cartoons of the First World War' *History Today*, August 1992, vol. 42, pp. 23–30.

10 L. Flood: *France 1914–18: Public Opinion and the War Effort* (London 1990), p. 57.

11 Quoted in F. Kupferman: 'Rumours, Fibs and Propaganda', *L'Histoire*, January 1988, p. 101.

12 C. Haste: op. cit., pp. 90–3.

13 H.F. Jahn: *Patriotic Culture in Russia during World War I* (New York 1995), p. 171.

14 J.M. Winter: *The Experience of World War One* (Oxford 1988), p. 186.
15 J. Williams: *The Home Fronts: Britain, France and Germany 1914–1918* (London 1972), p. 210.
Source A: F.A. Golder (ed.): *Documents of Russian History, 1914–1917* (London 1927), p. 192.
Source B: ibid., p. 195.
Source C: quoted in C. Haste: op. cit., pp. 56–7.
Source D: quoted in A. Marwick: *The Deluge*, op. cit., p. 82.
Source E: quoted in G. Hardach: 'Industrial Mobilisation in 1914–1918' in P. Fridenson (ed.): *The French Home Front 1914–1918* (Oxford 1992), p. 61.
Source F: G.F. Feldman: *Army, Industry and Labour in Germany 1914–1918* (Oxford 1992), pp. 535–41
Source G: quoted in J. Winter: *The Experience of World War I*, op. cit., p. 169.
Source H: quoted in J. Laver: *Imperial and Weimar Germany 1890–1933* (Cambridge 1992), p. 17.
Source I: quoted in A.J. Plotke: op. cit.
Source J: quoted in J. Laver: op. cit., p. 23.
Source K: quoted in A.J. Plotke: op. cit.
Source L: R. Graves: *Goodbye to All That* (London 1930), p. 59.
Source M: A. Hitler: *Mein Kampf* (Berlin 1925), p. 167.

3. TOTAL WAR – ECONOMIC MOBILISATION AND THE WAR ECONOMY

1   Quoted in J. Williams: op. cit., p. 47.
2   R. Chickering: *Imperial Germany and the Great War, 1914–1918* (Cambridge 1998), p. 39.
3   J. Williams: op. cit., p. 49.
4   S. Pollard: *The Development of the British Economy, 1914–1990* (London 1992), pp. 44–5.
5   The journal *Birzheve Vedomsti*, cited in L. Siegelbaum: *The Politics of Industrial Mobilisation in Russia* (London 1983), p. 21.
6   G. Hardach: *The First World War* (Harmondsworth 1977), p. 103.
7   R. Chickering: op. cit., p. 35.
8   Ibid., p. 38.
9   J.F. Godfrey: op. cit., p. 48.
10 G. Hardach in P. Fridenson (ed.): op. cit., pp. 78–9.
11 Quoted in W.B. Lincoln: op. cit., p. 191.
12 Quoted in L. Siegelbaum: op. cit., p. 41.
13 N. Stone: op. cit., pp. 298–9.
14 P. Kennedy: op. cit., pp. 262–3.

15 M.T. Florinsky: *The End of the Russian Empire* (New York 1961), p. 33.
16 P.A. Kharitonov in January 1915, quoted in ibid., p. 32.
17 A.J. Shingarev, quoted in ibid., p. 39.
18 Quoted in H.-U. Wehler: *The German Empire* (London 1985), p. 202.
19 P. Bernard and H. Dubief: *The Decline of the Third Republic* (Cambridge 1985), p. 28.
20 Col. A. Knox: op. cit., p. 171.
21 J. Winter: 'Some Paradoxes of the First World War' in J. Winter and R. Wall (eds): *The Upheaval of War* (Cambridge 1988), p. 10.
22 A. Offer: *The First World War: An Agrarian Interpretation* (Oxford 1989), p. 25.
23 Quoted in ibid., p. 28.
24 Quoted in H. Cowper *et al.*: op. cit., p. 165.
25 A. Grotjahn, writing in February 1915, quoted in H. Cecil and P.H. Liddle: *Facing Armageddon* (London 1996), p. 555.
26 A. Offer: op. cit., p. 45.
27 Ibid., p 71.
28 J. Kocka: op. cit., pp. 22–4.
29 S.G. Striumlin argues that even industrial wages declined, in real terms, from 22 roubles to 21. Cited in M.T. Florinsky: op. cit., p. 158.
30 Quoted in ibid., p. 128.
31 P. Bernard and H. Dubief: op. cit., p. 40.
32 L. Becker: *The Great War and the French People* (Leamington Spa 1985), pp. 126–7.
33 The *préfet* of Mazerolles, quoted in ibid., p. 121.
34 Ibid., p. 248.
35 P. Fridenson in J. Winter and J.-L. Robert (eds): op. cit., p. 244.
36 The *préfet* of Charente, quoted in L. Becker: op. cit., p. 21.
37 See K. Weller: *Don't Be a Soldier* (London 1985). According to Weller, wages rose, during 1914–18, by 75 per cent, prices by 105 per cent and food prices by 110 per cent.
38 Quoted in G. J. de Groot: op. cit., p. 119.
39 A. Triebel and P. Dewey, cited in R. Wall: 'English and German Families and the War' in J. Winter and R. Wall (eds): op. cit., p. 51. See also Triebel and Dewey's contributions to the same volume.
40 A. Offer: op. cit., p. 1.
Source A: from M. Shevin-Coetzee and F. Coetzee: op. cit., pp. 232–6.
Source B: J. Daborn: *Russia: Revolution and Counter-Revolution 1917–1924* (Cambridge 1991), pp. 34–5.
Source C: from P. Kennedy: op. cit., p. 345.
Source D: from R. Chickering: op. cit., p. 38.
Source E: from J. Winter in J. Winter and R. Wall (eds): op. cit., p. 40.
Source F: from E. Tobin: *War and the Working Class – the Case of Dusseldorf*, quoted in H. Cowper *et al.*: op. cit., p. 165.

Source G: from J. Williams: op. cit., p. 97.

Source H: from E. Blucher: *An English Wife in Berlin* (London 1920), p. 158.

Source I: quoted in A. Schlyapnikov: *On the Eve of 1917* (London 1982), p. 127.

Source J: from D. Koenker: *Moscow Workers In 1917*, cited in H. Cowper *et al.*: op. cit., p. 146.

Source K: M. Shevin-Coetzee and F. Coetzee: op. cit., pp. 242–7.

4. THE WOMEN'S WAR

1   A. Marwick: *Women at War, 1914–1918* (London 1977), pp. 83–90.

2   O. Figes: *A People's Tragedy* (London 1996), p. 419.

3   A. Marwick: *The Deluge*, op. cit., p. 92.

4   J.-L. Robert: 'Women and Work in France during the War' in J. Winter and R. Wall (eds): op. cit., p. 264.

5   From a postcard reprinted in ibid., p. 340

6   L.H. Edmondson: *Feminism in Russia, 1900–17* (London 1984), p. 162.

7   A.G. Meyer: 'The Impact of World War I' in B.E. Clements *et al.* (eds): *Russia's Women* (Berkeley 1991), p. 223.

8   U. Daniel: *The War from Within. German Working-Class Women in the First World War* (Oxford 1997), p. 45.

9   Quoted in ibid.: p. 248.

10 S. Boston: *Women Workers and the Trade Unions* (London 1980), p. 127.

11 P. Bartley: Votes for Women 1860–1928 (London 1998), p. 90.

12 H.L. Smith: *The British Women's Suffrage Campaign, 1866–1928* (London 1998), p. 55.

13 J.E. McMillan: *Housewife or Harlot?* (London 1981), p. 178.

14 Quoted in O. Figes: op. cit., p. 358.

15 R.J. Evans: *The Feminist Movement in Germany 1894–1933* (London 1976), p. 230.

Source A: M. Shevin-Coetzee and F. Coetzee: op. cit., p. 223

Source B: ibid., pp. 228–9.

Source C: F.H. Phillips (ed.): *Women and the Labour Party* (London 1918), p. 18.

Source D: M. Shevin-Coetzee and F. Coetzee: op. cit., p. 242.

Source E: *The Woman Worker* (21 March 1916).

Source F: from A. Marwick: *The Deluge*, op. cit., p. 92.

Source G: from S. Hause: 'More Minerva than Mars: The French Women's Rights Campaign and the First World War' in M.R. Higonnet *et al.* (eds): *Behind the Lines: Gender and the Two World Wars* (New Haven 1987), p. 102.

Source H: from D. Thom: 'The Bundle of Sticks' in A. John (ed.): *Unequal Opportunities* (Oxford 1986), p. 281.

Source I: quoted in M. Pugh: *Women and the Women's Movement in Britain 1914–1959* (London 1992), p. 8.

Source J: quoted in M. Shevin-Coetzee and F. Coetzee: op. cit., p. 251.

Source K: U. Daniel: op. cit., pp. 237–8.

Source L: quoted in L. Edmondson: op. cit., p. 166.

Source M: M. Shevin-Coetzee and F. Coetzee: op. cit., p. 260.

Source N: quoted in F. Gordon: *The Integral Feminist: Madeleine Pelletier* (Cambridge 1990), p. 247.

5. THE CHANGING ROLE OF GOVERNMENT

1 Quoted in W.B. Lincoln: op. cit., p. 195.

2 Ibid. p. 195.

3 Quoted in O. Figes: op. cit., p. 275.

4 Quoted in P. Bernard and H. Dubief: op. cit., p. 32.

5 Forain's cartoon, cited in L. Becker: op. cit., p. 323.

6 J.F. Godfrey: op. cit., p. 185.

7 G. D. Feldman: *Army, Industry and Labour in Germany 1914–1918* (Oxford 1992), p. 385.

8 G. Bordiugov: 'The First World War and Social Deviance in Russia' in H. Cecil and P.H. Liddle (eds): op. cit., p. 550.

Source A: quoted in G. A. Craig: *Germany 1866–1945* (Oxford 1981), p. 373.

Source B: quoted in G.R. Feldman: op. cit., p. 191.

Source C: quoted in K. H. Jarausch: *The Enigmatic Chancellor* (London 1973), p. 300.

Source D: quoted in B. Pares: *Letters of the Tsaritsa to the Tsar, 1914–1916* (London 1923), p. 110.

Source E: quoted in F.A. Golder (ed.): op. cit., p. 209.

Source F: from the *Observer*, December 1916.

Source G: quoted in D.R. Watson: *Georges Clemenceau: A Political Biography* (London 1974), p. 254.

Source H: quoted in M. Shevin-Coetzee and F. Coetzee: op. cit., p. 182.

Source I: quoted in A. Marwick: *The Deluge*, op. cit., p. 66.

Source J: quoted in ibid., p. 169.

Source K: quoted in F.A. Golder (ed.): op. cit., pp. 124–5.

Source L: quoted in A. Marwick: *The Deluge*, op. cit., p. 173.

Source M: quoted in ibid., p. 274.

6. PROTEST AND PACIFISM

1   See D. Gill and G. Dallas: 'Mutiny at Etaples Base in 1917', *Past and Present* 69 (1975), pp. 88–112.

2   'Jusqu'au bout-ism' refers to the determination to resist Germany until the last German had been expelled from French soil. See P. Flood: op. cit., pp. 147–78.

3   J.J. Becker: op. cit., p. 80.

4   Ibid., p. 197.

5   Ibid., p. 134.

6   Parisian letter monitored by Bordeaux censors, cited in ibid., p. 221.

7   See K. Weller: op. cit., for more on the activities of these tiny socialist groups during the war.

8   J.M. Winter: *The Experience of World War One*, op. cit., p. 159.

9   G.J. de Groot: op. cit., p. 141.

10 S. Pankhurst: *The Home Front* (London 1987), pp. 314–15.

11 J. Williams: op. cit., pp. 270–1.

12 Cited in P. Flood: op. cit., p. 160.

13 See H. Hafkesbrink: *Unknown Germany* (New Haven 1948), a digest of German soldiers' writings from the war.

14 J. Williams: op. cit., p. 238.

15 F. Zuckermann 'The Political Police, War and Society in Russia' in F. Coetzee and M. Shevin-Coetzee (eds): *Authority, Identity and the Social History of the Great War* (Oxford 1995), p. 40.

16 Ibid., p. 51.

17 Ibid.

Source A: from *The Times History of the War, Vol. 9* (London 1916), p 380.

Source B: from J. Kocka: op. cit., p. 61.

Source C: quoted in J. J. Becker: op. cit., p. 209.

Source D: G. Pedroncini, quoted in ibid., p. 217.

Source E: J. Maxton, cited in M. Shevin-Coetzee and F. Coetzee: op. cit., pp. 260–1

Source F: quoted in S. Hynes: *A War Imagined* (London 1990), pp. 174–5.

Source G: quoted in J. Hite: *Tsarist Russia* (London 1991), p. 78.

Source H: from H. Cowper *et al*.: op. cit., p. 147.

Source I: from M. Shevin-Coetzee and F. Coetzee: op. cit., pp. 291–2.

Source J: L. Trotsky: *The History of the Russian Revolution* (London 1965), pp. 42–3.

Source K: quoted in M. McCauley: *Octobrists to Bolsheviks* (London 1984) pp. 88–9.

7. THE FALL OF THE RUSSIAN AND GERMAN GOVERNMENTS

1   P. Lyaschenko, quoted in A.E. Adams (eds): *The Russian Revolution and Bolshevik Victory: Causes and Processes*, 2nd edn (Lexington 1972), p. xvii.
2   S. Fitzpatrick: *The Russian Revolution* (Oxford 1982), p. 33.
3   R. Pipes: *The Russian Revolution, 1899–1919* (London 1990), p. 192.
4   N. Stone: op. cit., pp. 148–9.
5   C. Read: *From Tsar to Soviets* (London 1996), p. 44.
6   See, for example, F. Zuckermann in F. Coetzee and M. Shevin-Coetzee (eds): op. cit., and L. Siegelbaum: op. cit.
7   Quoted in W. Lincoln: op. cit., p. 312.
8   Diane Koenker, quoted in C. Read: op. cit., p. 72.
9   Steve Smith, quoted in ibid., p. 72.
10 Quoted in R. Pipes: op. cit., p. 276.
11 E.H. Carr: *The Bolshevik Revolution: Volume 1* (Harmondsworth 1966), p. 81.
12 L. Kochan: *Russia in Revolution* (London 1966), p. 352.
13 V. Bulgakov: 'A Nation at War – the Russian Experience' in H. Cecil and P. H. Liddle (eds): op. cit., p. 541.
14 P. Kennedy: op. cit., pp. 268–9.
15 A. Offer: op. cit., p. 76.
16 Quoted in J. Kocka: op. cit., p. 156.
17 Ibid.
18 Quoted in R. Bessel: *Germany after the First World War* (Oxford 1993), p. 42.
19 J. Kocka: op. cit., p. 158.
20 Ibid., p. 159.
21 B. Davis: 'State and Society: Provisioning Berlin' cited by A. Jackson in H. Cecil and P.H. Liddle (eds): op. cit., p. 574.
22 Quoted in R. Bessel: op. cit., p. 44.
23 Ibid., pp. 47–8.
24 See J. Kocka: op. cit., and G. Feldman: op. cit.
Source A: quoted in L. Kochan and R. Abraham: *The Making of Modern Russia* (London 1983), p. 285.
Source B: R. Pipes: op. cit., p. 244.
Source C: quoted in J. Hite: op. cit., p. 81.
Source D: quoted in I. Porter and I. Armour: *Imperial Germany* (London 1991), pp. 105–6.
Source E: R. Bessel: op. cit., p. 46.
Source F: quoted in S. Lee: *Imperial Germany* (London 1999), p. 115.
Source G: quoted in M. McCauley: op. cit., pp. 90–1.
Source H: M. P. Price: *Dispatches from the Revolution* (ed. T. Rose) (Durham 1998), pp. 23–4.

Source I: quoted in J. Daborn: op. cit., p. 44.

Source J: quoted in A. Jackson: 'Germany: The Home Front' in H. Cecil and P.H. Liddle (eds): op. cit., p. 571.

Source K: from the diary of Colonel Hans Von Haeften, 6 November 1918.

8. VICTORY AND DEFEAT

1 P. Kennedy: op. cit., p. 259.
2 Ibid., p. 260.
3 A. Horne (ed.): op. cit., p. 4.
4 Quoted in A. Marwick: *War and Social Change in the Twentieth Century*, op. cit., p. 32.
5 A. Offer: op. cit., p. 23.
6 H.U. Wehler: op. cit., p. 203.
7 R. Chickering: op. cit., p. 179.
8 P. Kennedy: op. cit., p. 352.
9 J. Winter in 'Some Paradoxes of the First World War' in J. Winter and R. Wall (eds): op. cit., p. 40.
10 J. Winter: op. cit., p. 38.
11 A. Horne (ed.): op. cit., p. 2.
12 A. Offer: op. cit., p. 23.
13 See Source G below.
14 See J. Winter: *The Great War and the British People* (London 1986), ch. 8, for more detailed information on the demographic aftermath of the war in Britain.
15 J. Chastanet in February 1917, quoted by P. Flood: op. cit., p. 118.
16 See P. Pierrard: 'Lille: Ville Allemand' in *L'Histoire* (no. 107, January 1988), pp. 112–16.
17 G. Hardach: op. cit., p. 288.
18 J. Stevenson: *British Society 1914–1945* (London 1984), p. 106.
19 The League of Nations Memorandum on Production and Trade, 1928, quoted in G. Hardach: op. cit., pp. 287–9.
20 G. Kennan: *The Decline of Bismarck's European Order* (Princeton 1979), p. 3.

Source A: from P. Kennedy: op. cit., pp. 333 and 350.

Source B: from ibid., p. 354.

Source C: from R. Chickering: op. cit., p. 179.

Source D: quoted in R.B. Asprey: op. cit., p. 300.

Source E: J. Williams: op. cit., p. 290.

Source F: R. Chickering: op. cit., pp. 200–2.

Source G: H. Cowper *et al.*: op. cit., p. 36.

Source H: P. Kennedy: op. cit., p. 361.

Source I: A. Tardieu: 'The Policy of France' in *Foreign Affairs*, 1922, pp. 12–13.

Source J: P. Kennedy: op. cit., pp. 367–8.

Source K: quoted in B. Gardner (ed.): *Up the Line to Death: The War Poets 1914–1918* (London 1976), p. 148.

Source L: W. Langsam: *Documents and Readings in the History of Europe since 1918* (New York 1969), p. 273.

BIBLIOGRAPHY

Whilst there is an enormous literature on the First World War, much of this has traditionally been associated with the military campaigns and the experience of front-line soldiers. However, in recent years, there has been a welcome and overdue blossoming in studies of the social and economic dimensions of the conflict, and the centrality of the Home Front in the outcome of the war has come to be appreciated, as has the complex inter-relationship between the military and the domestic dimensions. Honourable mention in encouraging this trend must go to the publishers Berg, whose publication of a series of studies on the political economy of war and its social dimension has filled a number of gaps in the English language historiography of the subject.

This select bibliography includes primarily the main works referred to in compiling this book.

PRIMARY SOURCES

Probably the best available collection is M. Shevin-Coetzee and F. Coetzee (eds): *World War One and European Society* (Lexington 1995). Published to tie in with an Open University module, A. Marwick and W. Simpson (eds): *War, Peace and Social Change – Europe 1900–1955 – Documents I: 1900–1929* (Buckingham 1990) has some useful extracts. Also useful, although hard to find, is H. Hafkesbrink: *Unknown Germany* (London and New Haven 1948). On Russia, M. McCauley: *Octobrists to Bolsheviks* (London 1984) has a valuable section on the war, and M.P. Price (ed. T. Rose):

Dispatches from the Revolution (Durham 1998) is an interesting read on Russia.

SECONDARY SOURCES

There are numerous general histories of the First World War. Particularly accessible are M. Gilbert: *The First World War* (London 1994), J. Keegan: *The First World War* (London 1998) and A.J.P. Taylor: *The First World War* (London 1974). P. Liddle and H. Cecil (eds): Facing Armageddon (London 1996) contains a stimulating collection of essays on every aspect of the war.

Comparative accounts of the war, although few, are becoming more popular, the ground-breaking studies being J. Williams: *The Home Fronts* (London 1972) and P. Kennedy: *The Rise and Fall of the Great Powers* (London 1989), which has an important chapter on the conflict, comparing the relative performance of the Great Powers. Also worth reading for this approach are G. Hardach's marxist interpretation: *The First World War* (London 1977), A. Marwick: *War and Social Change in the 20th Century* (London 1974), H. Cowper *et al.*: *World War One and Its Consequences* (Buckingham 1990), J. Winter: *The Experience of World War One* (London 1988), J. Horne (ed.): *State, Society and Mobilisation in Europe during the First World War* (Cambridge 1997), and J. Winter and J.-L. Robert: *Capital Cities at War* (Cambridge 1998).

Specific countries have enjoyed rather varied treatment. On Germany, R. Chickering: *Imperial Germany and the Great War, 1914–1918* (Cambridge 1998) is quite excellent. See also the final chapter of H.-U. Wehler: *The German Empire* (Leamington Spa 1985). P. Bernard and H. Dubief: *The Decline of the Third Republic* (Cambridge 1985) includes a useful section on the First World War in France. On Russia, B. Lincoln: *Passage through Armageddon* (New York 1986), N. Stone: *The Eastern Front, 1914–1917* (London 1975) and M. Florinsky: *The End of Imperial Russia* (New York 1961) are of value, as is R. Pipes: *The Russian Revolution, 1899–1919* (London 1990).

For Britain, G. de Groot: *Blighty* (London 1996) and the very influential A. Marwick: *The Deluge* (London 1965) are possibly the most readable studies. J.M. Winter: *The Great War and the British People* (London 1986) and S. Constantine (ed.): *Britain and the First World War* (London 1995) should also be considered. T. Wilson's *The Myriad Faces of War* (Oxford 1985) may seem rather daunting, but it contains some fascinating details.

On the economic and financial dimension of the war, G. Feldman: *Army, Industry and Labour in Germany 1914–1918* (Oxford 1992) is almost definitive on Germany. See also: A. Offer: *The First World War: An Agrarian Interpretation* (Oxford 1989), L. Siegelbaum: *The Politics of Industrial Mobilisation in Russia 1914–1917* (London 1983), P. Gatrell: *The Tsarist Economy 1850–1917* (London 1986), J. Godfrey: *Capitalism at War* (Leamington Spa 1987), S. Pollard: *The Development of the British Economy, 1914–1990* (London 1992).

The recent upsurge of interest in the social impact of the conflict has led to the appearance of many important studies. These include: J.J. Becker: *The Great War and the French People* (Leamington Spa 1985), P. Fridenson (ed.): *The French Home Front* (Oxford 1992), J. Kocka: *Facing Total War* (Leamington Spa 1984), P. Flood: *France 1914–1918: Public Opinion and the War Effort* (London 1990), R. Wall and J. Winter: *Upheaval of War: Family Work and Welfare in Europe 1914–18* (Cambridge 1988), U. Daniel: *The War from Within* (Oxford 1997), R. Bessel: *Germany after the First World War* (Oxford 1993), F. Coetzee and M. Shevin-Coetzee: *Authority, Identity and the Social History of the Great War* (Oxford 1995). The French journal *L'Histoire* in January 1988 contained a series of interesting articles on social themes, including P. Pierrard: *Lille: Ville Allemand*, and F. Thebaud: *Femmes et Etrangers en Travail*.

On the politics of the war and the revolutions in Russia and Germany there has, of course, been much written. Worth examination are C. Read: *From Tsar To Soviets: The Russian People and their Revolution* (London 1996), A.E. Adams (ed.): *The Russian Revolution and Bolshevik Victory: Causes and Processes*, 2nd edn (Lexington 1972), S. Fitzpatrick: *The Russian Revolution* (Oxford 1982), H. Rogger: *Russia in the Age of Modernisation and Revolution, 1881–1917* (London 1983), E.H. Carr: *The Bolshevik Revolution, Volume 1* (Harmondsworth 1966), L. Kochan: *Russia in Revolution* (London 1966), L. Kochan and R. Abraham: *The Making of Modern Russia* (London 1983), K. Weller: *Don't Be a Soldier* (London 1985), J. Bourne: *Britain and the Great War 1914–1918* (London 1989), J. Turner:

Britain and the First World War (London 1988), R.B. Asprey: *The German High Command at War: Hindenburg and Ludendorff and the First World War* (London 1991), I. Porter and I. Armour: *Imperial Germany* (London 1991). Also, in *L'Histoire* in January 1988, F. Kupferman: *Rumeurs, Bobards et Propagande* is an interesting read.

INDEX